THE MODERN
BUSINESS LETTER
WRITER'S MANUAL

THE MODERN BUSINESS LETTER WRITER'S MANUAL

Marjane Cloke
and
Robert Wallace

Dolphin Books
Doubleday & Company, Inc., Garden City, New York

Dedicated to—

The late Richard H. Morris, whose patient teachings and generously shared knowledge made this book possible.

Marjane and Bob

Library of Congress Cataloging in Publication Data

Cloke, Marjane.
  The modern business letter writer's manual.
  1. Commercial correspondence—Handbooks, manuals, etc. I.
Wallace, Robert, 1940–   joint author. II. Title.
HF5721.C53 1974   651.7'5
ISBN: 0-385-06952-9
Library of Congress Catalog Card Number 73–14653
Dolphin Books edition: 1974

Originally published by Doubleday & Company, Inc., in 1969

ACKNOWLEDGMENTS

No book is really written by the authors alone. It takes help from many wonderful people. We'd like to thank those who added so much—knowingly and unknowingly—to our story.

For his editorial guidance—

John P. Brion

For their contributions—

Howard Barnhill, Carol Brownstein, Angela Coccia, Joseph Engelman, Pat Hoerman, Henry Hayden, Lou Kriloff, Maureen Kapherr, Michael McNamara, Patrick McGinty, Betsy Maloney, Peter R. Neuman, Iver Olsen, Irene Schultz, John Sargent, Martel Schoenblum, Ruth Schaefer, Bob Vitagliano, Jack Webb, Sam Warriner

For their patience and understanding—

Our Spouses
Bob and Betsy

Contents

Dear Letter Writer:

No one in the world can write a better letter for you than you can write for yourself . . . because no one thinks exactly like you, talks like you, or reacts like you.

If your letters are an expression of your personality—if they say what you think and what you wish them to say—they are good letters.

Of course, wishing alone won't make your letters good. But if you keep some simple guidelines in mind, and apply what follows in this book, you may be surprised how easily you can write really excellent letters.

Good writing!

THE AUTHORS

LETTER WRITER'S TEN COMMANDMENTS

1. It will LOOK EASY to read.

2. It will get off to a fast, interesting and appropriate start.

3. It will get to the point quickly.

4. It will be CLEAR and CONCISE—say what has to be said in as few words as possible without being curt—avoid unfamiliar phraseology.

5. It will be easy and interesting to read—points follow in natural sequence—avoids nonstop sentences—contains no tiresome repetition.

6. It will be COMPLETE—tell reader all he wants to know or should be told.

7. It will refrain from giving unnecessary detail and stating the obvious.

8. It will be friendly, considerate and tactful—and will play up the reader's interest and problems.

9. It will motivate the reader to do, think or feel as I wish him to.

10. It will have an appropriate close.

Introduction

THINGS TO THINK ABOUT

Every day we read and hear how rapidly things are changing. Technology appears to have taken over the world: a theory two years old, and still valid, is classical; mobility, constant change are expected and looked forward to. It is the rule.

And writing is no exception to the rule. Rummage through your attic (if your house *has* an attic) and find an old letter. It's a good bet you'll be surprised how different it is from letters written today—by some people. It may even be a bigger surprise to know that many people are *still* writing that way, though they wouldn't dream of talking that way.

Good letters today are much like conversation. The rules we learned or failed by in school are being broken. In fact, in this book you'll find no rules to hang your hat—or our necks—on. Just ideas that can help you write more up-to-the-minute, interesting, and expressive letters.

Sentences are being started with conjunctions and ended with prepositions. Words are coined and contracted . . . the sacred infinitive is being unmercifully split. Dots and dashes are used as alternates to commas, colons and semi-colons.

The stilted, stuffy "business" style is old stuff. Businessmen, after all, are human and more and more of them admit it by the way they write.

Writing isn't easy for some people; but that can be overcome. In fact, a large part of the solution is to forget about having to sound a certain way—about having to adopt a certain style—and just be natural.

It helps, too, to know some of the reasons why intelligent, capable people write bad letters so that you can avoid making the same mistake for the same reasons:

They . . .

▶give in to pressures of work and don't plan a letter properly before writing. Common errors result in omission of important points, disorganization and probably confusion in the mind of the person who gets the letter.

Never forget—*a letter means just what your reader thinks it means*—whether or not that's what you intended. Communication is a two-way process—what you say and what the other person hears or reads.

▶fall into a rut. You may not hear the crash, but if all your letters sound the same—use the same openings, closings and phrases—there's a good chance they won't get the action you want because they indicate you aren't thinking about what you are saying.

▶refuse to write as naturally as they speak. This results in rigid-sounding prose lacking the sincerity people respond to.

▶lack courage—are unwilling to stick a neck out and say something original for fear it won't be legally correct or will be badly taken.

The alternate is to quote directly from a contract or someone else's phraseology (the boss's, for example) which is firm ground. The problem is these sources seldom say *what you want to say*. They never say it *the way you would say it*.

►assume a conversational style of writing is undignified in business communication. There is nothing undignified about being natural. Also, there is nothing dignified about being stuffy.

For some people, avoiding these problems means forgetting everything they have learned about business writing. Aside from being a good idea on occasion, forgetting is easy. Pull out your pocket watch—wave it in front of your eyes. You are hypnotized. You will forget. You will only remember these new, easy rules:

►write as you talk, in a natural, conversational tone.

►be yourself. Don't try to imitate anyone else's style.

►write to express—not impress. Use words that are easily understood and stay away from technical terms. Never use a big word when a smaller one will do.

►use your imagination. Find new ways to say those "same old things."

►be sincere. Be friendly. Let people know that being of service is a pleasure not a chore.

►use live words, not dead ones; active verbs, not passive ones.

►play up your reader's interests, and play down the company's. Write in terms of "you," not "we."

►remember letter writing is the art of impressing and influencing the emotions of other people just as in advertising, selling or any other form of human persuasion.

1.

Plan before you write

Habit may well be one of the most powerful forces on earth. When you take a busy man who has a thousand things to do, twice that many to think about doing, and give him a letter to write, it's going to read with all the excitement of a telephone directory. He'll lean on phrases he has used before, write words he's not fully concentrating on, get the job done as quickly as possible and forget it.

And there is a pretty good chance the person getting the letter written under those circumstances will forget it too. That is, assuming he reads it at all!

Too many people treat letters like those "bad pennies" that keep turning up even when you concentrate on avoiding them. It's a shame, because letters offer a beautiful opportunity to make a good impression on other people—and have them think well both of the writer and his company.

But making that kind of impression takes thought; it won't just happen automatically when the letter is finished and mailed. Once you have established a pattern of thinking out a letter *before* you start writing, your letters will improve—and writing will be more fun and take less effort.

Here are some guidelines.

►Make sure you have all the details about the situation your letter will cover.

►Know the main reason you're writing. Sound stupid? Well, consider: is your letter to cool off an angry complainer, to quote a price, to say no to a request? Whatever the main reason, have it firmly in mind *before writing*—aim at getting it into the letter as soon as possible—and *make it clear*.

►Is there another purpose the letter should accomplish? If you quote a price, should you also make a bid for the order? If you turn down a request, should you suggest an alternate course of action? And an angry complainer has to be won back as well as cooled off. Know how the situation is to be handled before you write the first word.

►If your letter is to lead to a direct action, be sure you say what it is, and how soon it should be taken.

►Before you do anything, set aside specific time for handling your correspondence—time when you will not be interrupted. Good planning requires concentration.

We suggest the first hour in the morning. Phones seldom ring—and guests seldom visit that early. And your thoughts are sharper first thing; they haven't yet been cluttered with the day's problems.

►Write notes to yourself when you plan, but don't write the letter until you've phrased it in your mind. That way you'll avoid using words and phrases that are unnatural.

In developing a Letterwriting Training Program for Mutual Of New York (one of the largest life and health insurance companies), we put together PLAN SHEETS. They act as a guide to all the thoughts you should have clear in your mind before you get one word on paper.

When we first got the idea of these sheets, hundreds and hundreds of letters were studied, and we discovered a surprising thing. There really are only three different kinds of letters we write—one we originate; a reply to another; and a follow-up. And so we fashioned three PLAN SHEETS.

Once you have filled out your PLAN SHEET, your letter is practically written—and you are not apt to forget anything which should be included.

For instance, you have just received this letter:

                                                            Date

Gentlemen:

Although I address this letter "Gentlemen," I'm not so sure you are. When I find out that you have had men talking with my neighbors, my bank, probably even my tailor to find out what kind of guy I am—I doubt seriously that you are gentlemen.

I filled out all the questions your agent asked—and truthfully. Why do you have to check up with everyone else about me?

You had better have a good explanation—or else you can tell your agent he can keep the policy. I don't want it.

                                                    Joseph Street

Angry? You bet. And your job is to write Mr. Street. Certainly you wouldn't want to tackle this answer without having planned it well! But before filling out the PLAN SHEET FOR REPLIES, turn to the top of page 18 for your facts.

PLAN SHEET FOR
REPLY TO A LETTER

1. WHAT IS PURPOSE OF MY LETTER?

Get new. client to accept policy

2. WHAT DOES WRITER WANT TO KNOW—OR HAVE US DO?

Why we checked on him

3. CAN WE GIVE READER THE INFORMATION—OR DO AS HE ASKS?

Yes

4. WHAT POINTS SHOULD I COVER IN MY LETTER?

1) *Reasons for investigations*

2) *Common practice*

3) *Results of our check-up*

4) *Hope he'll take policy*

5) _____

5. IS THERE ANY WAY THE READER BENEFITS?

By insuring only better applicants, we keep costs lower and dividends higher

6. WHAT APPROACH SHOULD MY LETTER TAKE?

Admission of Guilt   (Apologetic)   Appreciative

Arouse Curiosity   Ask for Help..Cooperation

Ask Question   (Awareness of Reader's Problem)

(Complimentary or Congratulatory)   Good News

Humorous   Personal   Positive vs Negative

Regretful   Sense of Urgency   Sympathetic

Because you may not be familiar with insurance practices, here is some background you would need in order to reply.

►On large policies, most life insurance companies conduct investigations into the prospect's financial, physical, moral and family background.

►The purpose, of course, is to confirm the facts given by the applicant; be certain the risk is a good one; be sure the applicant can carry this amount of insurance without a problem.

►By insuring the best prospects we can keep costs for insurance down, and pay better dividends.

►In this instance, Mr. Street applied for $20,000 and he did pass our inspection. Now we are ready to issue the policy.

OK? Let's work out the PLAN SHEET on the preceding page.

NOW . . . putting all those points together, here's our reply:

Date

Dear Mr. Street:

Your grocer Fred, George the tailor, Doc Jones, banker Bill and even Uncle Sam in Washington are all in agreement . . . you are an excellent prospect for insurance coverage.

You see, these are the people who know you best—the people who told us how fine an individual you are.

Since every life insurance company must protect its insureds and their investment, most of us investigate applicants in advance; and eliminate those who are poor insurance risks. Your application has been processed . . . and we find you to be a preferred risk. Our apologies for any concern our inquiry might have caused.

Thanks to your friends, we know you better and look forward to welcoming you as one of our nearly 2 million insureds.

Cordially,

Never realized difficult letters could be written so easily, did you? And so effectively, too.

PLAN SHEETS help in many ways:

►letters will be easier to understand

►they will contain *all* the important points

►all questions will be answered

►messages will invariably be shorter

Their greatest value is when you're dealing with a complicated problem—or a lengthy subject. Here they can be invaluable in helping you organize, sort and analyze your thoughts before you begin dictating or putting words on paper. There's another plus—planning ahead can help set the right tone to accomplish your purpose.

How about trying this same system to originate a letter?

The problem:

Your company is one of the largest department stores in the country. Consequently, the list of charge-account customers is tremendous. While you enclose return envelopes with bills, they are not stamped.

During any given year, you receive hundreds of letters from customers asking why such a large organization can't put a stamped envelope in with its bills.

Management has decided to prepare a standard letter which can be used to answer all such inquiries.

And, some background:

Your store mails approximately 3 million bills a year.

At 6¢ an envelope, it would cost approximately $180,000 additional to stamp the envelopes. And to offset this, it would mean increased costs on merchandise.

On the facing page, let's work through our PLAN SHEET FOR LETTERS ORIGINATED. Again, we'll work it through, together.

NOW . . . putting all those points together, here's our reply:

Date

6¢ isn't a big amount, Mr. Smith . . .

we'd be the first to agree. That is why we can readily understand your asking us to include a stamped return envelope with your charge notices.

But when you take the cost of putting a 6¢ stamp on each return envelope . . . multiply it by the more than 3 million bills that go out in a year . . . you have a figure of over, $180,000! And when you consider that our operating costs must go into the costs for our products, you can quickly see why, in these days of soaring costs, we don't want to saddle our customers with any extras.

We do want you to know how grateful we are for every suggestion that would enable us to give our customers better service. We appreciate your taking the time to send us yours.

Thank you,

**PLAN SHEET FOR
LETTERS ORIGINATED**

1. WHAT IS PRIMARY PURPOSE OF MY LETTER?

Advise reader of new policy on stamped envelopes

2. IS THERE A SECOND PURPOSE?

Keep his business & good will

3. WHAT DO I WANT THE READER TO KNOW — OR DO?

We won't put stamps on return envelopes

4. WHY?

Costs too much over year

5. HOW CAN READER BENEFIT?

Keeps cost of merchandise down

6. POINTS TO BE COVERED IN MY LETTER.

1) *Won't put stamps on envelopes*

2) *How many envelopes in year*

3) *What total cost would be*

4) *Effect on customers*

7. WHAT APPROACH SHOULD MY LETTER TAKE?

Admission of Guilt   Apologetic   (Appreciative)

Arouse Curiosity   Ask for Help.. Cooperation

Ask Question   (Awareness of Reader's Problem)

Complimentary or Congratulatory   Good News

Humorous   Personal   Positive vs Negative

(Regretful)   Sense of Urgency   Sympathetic

Another tough assignment handled with a minimum of trouble. Are you convinced these SHEETS save you work?

Ready to handle the third—and last—type letter? This should be a lot easier now that you're getting the knack of it.

The problem:

You've enlisted in the Air Force—and the only thing holding up your acceptance is a medical report that was requested of your personal physician.

Twice you've written . . twice there's been no reply. And time is running short for you. This letter has to do the trick. Here's where the PLAN SHEET on the facing page will help.

Would you send those records, if you received this follow-up?

Dear Doctor:

Is my heart bad?

Do I have an ailment I'm not aware of?

Medically, don't I meet the Air Force requirements?

These are just a few of the questions going thru my mind, Doctor Melvin . . since I haven't received the medical report I asked you for. Won't you put my mind at ease, and also help me get into the Air Force?

You must be very busy, but if the Air Force doesn't have my medical record by next Friday, they won't accept me.

Please, take just a few minutes now, to have your nurse put my records together and mail them at once. I'm anxious to get in the service and do my part.

Thank you,

PLAN SHEET FOR
FOLLOW—UP

1. WHAT DO I WANT READER TO DO?

Send medical report

2. WHAT LIKELY REASONS WOULD READER HAVE FOR NOT HAVING DONE THIS?

Too busy - Away - Didn't receive previous request

3. WHAT APPEAL CAN I MAKE TO GET ACTION?

Might lose my chance to get in Air Force

Show concern about my medical record

4. HOW CAN I PHRASE MY APPROACH TO MAKE IT MORE ATTENTION—GETTING? WHAT TECHNIQUE COULD I USE?

Ask question - show concern

5. POINTS TO COVER.

1) *What I need from doctor*
2) *Why I need it*
3) *How fast I need it*
4) *Please send it*

6. WHAT APPROACH SHOULD LETTER TAKE?

Admission of Guilt   Apologetic   Appreciative

   Arouse Curiosity   (Ask for Help..Cooperation)

Ask Question   (Awareness of Reader's Problem)

   Complimentary or Congratulatory   Good News

Humorous   Personal   Positive vs Negative

   Regretful   (Sense of Urgency)   Sympathetic

Let's be realistic. Planning this way takes time . . . and you wouldn't make a PLAN SHEET out for every letter you needed to write. Just the difficult ones. But it may pay dividends while you're trying to school yourself to plan all your messages this way for a while.

It won't take long before you have these questions established firmly in mind, and automatically you'll ask them before you begin to dictate. And then you can reserve actually filling out such SHEETS for those really complicated messages—messages which require considerable tact to write perfectly.

Having done all the things we've talked about, put yourself into the shoes of the person you're writing to and test your reaction. If you still wear a smile when you're done, you have probably written a darn good letter.

Just remember, like everything successful in life—PLAN FIRST!

2.

In the beginning

If you are familiar with advertising, you're aware of the importance of the headline in an ad. It is the opening sentence or phrase which has the responsibility of gaining the reader's attention.

The opening of a letter has the same responsibility . . . for if the opening doesn't create interest, chances are the rest of the letter won't get read.

Yet, it's remarkable how many letters get off to dull, uninteresting starts which seriously impair, if not destroy, the chances of the rest of the letter accomplishing its aim. People seem to stumble over the openings of their letters, and after that you can almost see them sprawled over the remainder of the page.

The opening of a letter is as important as any personal introduction to another person. It will be judged—and you will be judged—by the impression it makes. A bad or inappropriate opening is like a weak handshake and will be judged just as negatively.

Conversely, a good opening will put your reader in a receptive frame of mind for the rest of your message . . . and considerably improve your chances of achieving what you set out to achieve.

We could give you lists of things to avoid—such as:

Don't begin by telling your reader what he already knows

Dear Mr. Jones:

We have your letter of May 3 asking us if we could send 10,000 books to you.

Yes, we can supply 10,000 books to you and they will go out soon.

(The whole first paragraph repeats what your reader wrote to you. So you're wasting his and your time. Begin with the second. Just say . . .)

Dear Mr. Jones:

Yes, we can supply 10,000 books to you and they will go out soon.

or

Dear Mr. Bryon:

Thank you for your letter. The check we sent you on December 2 was in the amount of $140 for payment of the dividend on your policy.

You are right. We did send the incorrect amount of your dividend. It should have been $150—and the difference is going out to you today. I'm sorry.

(Wouldn't it sound better just to send the second paragraph?)

Dear Mr. Bryon:

You are right. We did send the incorrect amount for your dividend. It should have been $150—and the difference is going out to you today. I'm sorry.

Don't take too long getting to the point

Dear Tom:

The other day I met Bill Cool who told me he had been talking with your wife and learned that you had not been well this winter. So I am writing to ask how you are now.

(Need we say more? It would be so simple just to say . . .)

Dear Tom:

How are you? I've just heard you have been ill this winter.

or

American Airlines:

There have been some administrative problems in our West Coast offices. And because it is my job to see they are taken care of, it is necessary for me to make a trip to California next month. Can you tell me the times of your flights to San Francisco, daily?

(Wouldn't American Airlines rather get . . .)

American Airlines:

Please send me a list of your daily flights to San Francisco during the coming month.

(Only takes the reader a minute to know what you want, when you write this way.)

Don't tell your reader he failed, or neglected to do something —or made a mistake

Dear Mr. Walker:

You neglected to include your check for the books you ordered from us. We cannot release them until we have the money in hand.

(Wouldn't it be nicer to let him save face? Like . . .)

Dear Mr. Walker:

We're delighted to get your order for the books. Unfortunately, the check was not included. But just as soon as it is received, the books will be on their way to you.

or

Dear Mrs. Newman:

You failed to tell us in your letter when you need the material you ordered from us. And we can't tell you if it will be available until we know when it must be delivered.

(After that, I'd go to another store. It would be just as easy— and nicer—to say . . .)

Dear Mrs. Newman:

We're very anxious to supply you with the material you ordered. Could you let me know the date it is needed, so I can see if it will be in stock by then?

(Easy, isn't it? And it only takes a minute.)

Don't let openings sound blunt or tactless

Dear Miss Kapherr:

You told us you have not seen a doctor for the past 5 years. And we have just learned that you did.

(Aren't you, in effect, calling this woman a liar? Always give everyone the benefit of the doubt.)

Dear Miss Kapherr:

No one likes to remember unpleasant things. And I'm sure that is why you forgot about your visit to your doctor a few years ago.

or

Dear Mr. Wall:

We can't send you the information you requested. It would take too much time to gather it from all our records.

(I hope we don't ever need any information from Mr. Wall! We could have tried . . .)

Dear Mr. Wall:

Unfortunately, no where in our records do we have all the information you requested. I'm so sorry, I would like to have been able to help.

(Even though the reader didn't get it, bet he isn't half as angry with us—just because of the way we approached the problem.)

We'd much rather emphasize the positive, so here is a real list of DO's for openings:

**DO talk about "you"—not "I" or "we" . . . have an aware-
ness of the reader's situation or problem**

You have done an excellent job, John . . .

in making our product so well known in your town.

(rather than)

Dear John:

We have an excellent product and are glad that you are
selling it so well in your town.

or

When it comes to getting clients, Dick . . .

you certainly play a tremendous part in the success we've
had with ours. Your "know how" has helped us keep getting
larger and larger accounts each year.

(not)

Dear Dick:

Our Company now has some of the largest accounts in its
field. We have worked hard to obtain only the best, and our
policy on obtaining clients has proven management's theories
are right. I am glad you have done a good job in bringing
in accounts management considers worth having.

(We're all egotists at heart. We all like to be flattered. A
little goes a long way toward making people feel needed.)

DO take the opportunity to say something complimentary or congratulatory whenever possible

It's great, Pete!

I mean the news about your new position. It will just be that much more fun now to talk with you about some new equipment I want to order.

(*rather than*)

Dear Pete:

I am thinking of ordering some new equipment. Since you now have a higher position in your company, I thought I would talk with you about it.

(Cold? Disinterested? Sure sounds that way.)

` *or*

No one, but you, Charlie . . .

could have handled the Neverdull account so well. Your patience, over a long period, certainly paid off. I appreciate all you have done.

(*not*)

Dear Charlie:

I told you if you could just be patient for a while you would be able to handle the Neverdull account. I am glad to hear they are staying with us.

(Everyone likes to hear he's done a good job—regardless of who might have pointed him toward it.)

DO be appreciative

I can't thank you enough, Bob . . .

for the excellent job you did in getting our new EDP program off the ground. We are all set now, and ready to roll.

(*rather than*)

Dear Bob:

I guess you're glad our job on the EDP program is all finished. It certainly took some time and work. But now we're all set to put it in operation.

(Not even a little bit of credit?)

or

You were so nice, Mrs. Fixit . . .

to think of our store when you needed the material to finish off your playroom. And we are most appreciative of your inquiry. Here is the information.

(*rather than*)

Dear Mrs. Fixit:

Here is the information you need about material to finish off your playroom. When you have decided what you need, just let me know.

(Why? You don't even sound pleased I inquired.)

DO be positive—not negative

We're happy to tell you, Mr. Cane . . .

that many of your hospital costs will be paid by your policy. However, there will be some that are not covered.

(*rather than*)

Dear Mr. Cane:

We're sorry to tell you that we can only pay part of your hospital costs. They are not all covered under your policy.

(Under the top letter, I didn't feel so badly about not getting everything taken care of. But now—I'm annoyed.)

or

90% of your loan balance, Mr. Boro . . .

has been paid. You should be very pleased. May we have the balance of 10% by the 30th of next month? Thank you.

(*rather than*)

Dear Mr. Boro:

There is still 10% of your loan balance outstanding. I am sure you want to pay the entire balance, and we will expect it by the 30th of next month.

(Next time, I'll find that "friend at Chase Manhattan." Not this bank!)

DO point out the urgency of the situation

Time is running out, Mr. Fox . . .

We have just one week before the report is due on last quarter's sales results, and to complete it we need your figures.

(rather than)

Dear Mr. Fox:

As you know, our quarterly report on sales results is due on the 23rd. We would like to have your figures to add to the report.

(Anytime will do—at least it sounds that way.)

or

I know how anxious you are, Mrs. Smith . . .

to have your daughter's wedding reception in our Club. It's very popular for such affairs. And because of other inquiries, may I have your deposit by June 10—so we may assure you of having the date?

(rather than)

Dear Mrs. Smith:

You indicated you would very much like to reserve our Club for your daughter's wedding reception. As you can appreciate, that is a very popular time of year and several people have requested it for the same time. So may we have your deposit at your earliest convenience?

(My earliest convenience and yours could be entirely different things.)

DO make a statement that will arouse curiosity

Does your wife know about Grace, Mr. Hayden?

(rather than)

As you know, your insurance contract provides a 31 day grace period beyond the normal date your premium is due.

(Bet Mr. *and* Mrs. Hayden read the top one.)

or

Would you believe $1000, Jack?

$2000? $3500? Well, that's how much I can get you for your old car. Interested?

(rather than)

Dear Jack:

If you would be interested in turning in your present car for a new one, I believe we could offer you a trade-in value of $3500. Please let me know.

(Just ain't no comparison!)

DO ask questions

Did our original letter go astray, Mr. Dill?

(rather than)

Dear Mr. Dill:

We wrote you on January 4 and have had no answer.

(So?)

DO ask for help and cooperation

Would you be willing, Mr. Badger . . .

to take a few minutes to help with a problem concerning your merchandise?

(rather than)

Dear Mr. Badger:

We cannot ship the merchandise you ordered since there is a problem on which we need your help.

(It's nice to be needed—and most of us are only too glad to help.)

or

You're the answer, Mrs. Hill . . .

to the question of whether or not we can give you the paint you need for your living room. If you can wait 2 weeks . . . we'll have it. Otherwise, may I suggest you call the L. R. Paint Company.

(rather than)

Dear Mrs. Hill:

The paint you need for your living room is temporarily out of stock. We expect it in a few weeks.

(I can wait when someone asks so nicely—and gives me a definite time to expect it.)

DO admit when you're wrong

You are absolutely right, Mr. Taylor . . .

we did make a mistake in your bill and I apologize. A correct bill is attached.

(rather than)

Dear Mr. Taylor:

Your bill should have been for $20 instead of $25. We are sending you a corrected statement.

(We all love to catch people making mistakes. It's the sadist in us. And we're so smug when they admit it.)

or

I hang my head, Mr. Morris . . .

and ask you to forgive me for sending you the wrong costumes. The right ones are on their way, and I hope you haven't been too inconvenienced.

(rather than)

Dear Mr. Morris:

The 1843 period costumes are on their way, and we would appreciate it if you would have the others ready to be picked up when the truck arrives.

(I'd like to say, "You made the mistake. You get them ready.")

DO use identifying or notifying openings

Remember, Tracy . . .

that material on the Jones case you called me about last week? Well, here's an addition to the file that might shed more light!

(*rather than*)

Dear Tracy:

Enclosed find additional correspondence relating to that case we talked about last week.

(Presumably, there are many cases. How is your reader to know which?)

or

The blue chair, Mrs. Adele . . .

with the pale green pattern, which you looked at last week during our fall sale, is still unsold. You seemed so interested in it, I thought you would want to know.

(*rather than*)

Dear Mrs. Adele:

We still have a blue chair which has not been sold. You may be interested.

(It could be any blue chair—not necessarily the one in which I was interested.)

DO be sympathetic

Even though our acquaintance, Pitt . . .

has been through correspondence, I feel I know you, personally. If there is anything I can do from this end to ease your workload at this time, just let me know.

(rather than)

Dear Pitt:

Since you are having some personal problems at this time, can you tell me with whom I should get in touch about our work projects?

or

There's never a good time to be ill, Mr. Bones . . .

and I'm sorry to hear you are. I'm even more sorry to hear it spoiled your vacation plans!

Don't worry about the little job you were doing for me. It can certainly wait until you are well . . . and even until you get that vacation.

(rather than)

Dear Mr. Bones:

It will be all right if you can't finish my job right now while you are ill. But I would like to get it as soon as you get back to work.

DO use humor

Last—but far from least, is humor. It can be a builder-upper; but it can also be a dangerous toy. Approach it with caution. Remember, you don't have your facial expressions or tone of voice to put it over. It must stand on its own. So exercise judgment on this one!

You've confused me, Tom . . .

and that doesn't take much. But I'm really not sure if the elevation on Cedar or Maple Street is the one which needs repair.

(rather than)

Dear Tom:

I can't understand your letter. Which is the elevation which needs repair—the one on Cedar or the one on Maple Street?

or

You left one of your patients uncovered, Dr. Well . . .

Mr. Curt Rose's application for life insurance can't be acted on until we have your medical report. And, in the meantime, he doesn't have any insurance coverage.

(rather than)

Dear Dr. Well:

We are still waiting for your medical report on Mr. Curt Rose. Please send it to us at once so we can consider his application for life insurance.

Suppose we turn back for a few minutes to one of the letters we put together in Chapter I. On page 16—

> Mr. Street wrote to complain about having an investigation made about him.

Now back a few years ago (or possibly right before this book was bought) Mr. Street might have received a reply which began like this:

> Dear Mr. Street:
>
> Thank you for your letter telling us how upset you were when you found out about the investigation we made about you.

(This opening would have done a few things . . .

.. made Mr. Street angry all over again by reminding him he had been upset.

.. confirmed what he already thought . . . he had caught us sneaking around checking on his background.

.. made us look pretty silly thanking him for telling us we weren't gentlemen.)

Now applying the **DO**'s we've just studied, there are many ways of handling this situation. Here's how those **DO**'s influenced our answer.

When we worked out the Plan Sheet on page 17, we agreed the *purpose* of our reply was to get Mr. Street to accept our policy. And we felt we could accomplish this by making our letter sound apologetic . . . or complimentary . . . or congratulatory . . . or by showing an awareness of his problem.

So we've given ourselves several tacks to take. (We're not always so fortunate!) Let's put our imagination to work and try an opening for each—keeping in mind the *purpose* of our message.

DO be apologetic

I am so sorry we've seemed indiscreet, Mr. Street . . .

and hope after I've explained our reason for asking about you, you will forgive us.

(Would you be offended if you received this? Don't we all like to have someone apologize to us . . . and offer an explanation?)

Do show awareness of problem

Dear Mr. Street:

It's easy to understand how you feel—I felt just the same when the bank did a little checking on me before I bought my first car.

(You've put yourself right into the reader's place. Now you seem like a human being who understands why he is angry.)

DO be congratulatory

Congratulations, Mr. Street . . .

you've qualified with flying colors for the finest insurance coverage issued. I'm only sorry that in gathering our facts, we gave you some concern.

(We all like to hear we're eligible for the finest of anything. You can almost see Mr. Street's chest swelling with pride.)

DO be complimentary

Dear Mr. Street:

Your grocer Fred, George the tailor, Doc Jones, banker Bill and even Uncle Sam in Washington are all in agreement . . . you are an excellent prospect for insurance coverage.

(Remember page 18?)

A letter can begin many different ways—can be effective in many different ways—and can accomplish its mission in many different ways. And the key to its success is the word "different."

Make your openings "different." Use imagination! The success of any letter depends in large measure upon its opening. Spend time on them . . . think about them . . . and when you've got a good one, the remainder of the letter will follow logically and easily.

The particular opening you use will, of course, depend on what you want the letter to accomplish and to whom it is written.

There isn't any list of openings that can be applied to all situations. There isn't any foolproof formula. Good openings require thought. But if they create interest and place your reader in a receptive frame of mind to read and act on your letter, they are worth the extra few minutes it takes to think of them.

3.

In the middle

Believe it or not, there's a difference between the opening and middle of a letter—although the number of one paragraph letters going out these days would make it difficult to prove!

The opening is an important tool to get your reader's interest. Make him curious about what comes next. Sort of like the smell of the cheese that gets the mouse interested in the trap.

Once you have constructed the opening, break off and start on the body of the letter.

This is where you state your case—make the point you want to get across—substantiate any ideas or decisions—explain why what must be, must be.

This is the cheese the opening promised. And here are some characteristics of really good "cheese"!

CLEARNESS

A clear letter is one that says what you want to say, in a manner that can't possibly be misunderstood. Keep in mind that written communication involves not only what you write, but also what the reader reads—and they might be two entirely different things.

The words you use are the result of your education, experience, attitude, personality. The meaning the reader puts into those words depends on *his* education, experience, attitude and personality. When you plan a letter give some thought to what your reader may be like, and how much he knows about the subject. Also, *how much you want him to know*.

Obviously, each letter will have to be written to meet a precise set of circumstances, but there are some good general rules for getting clarity in your letters.

Avoid technical terms

Especially if you're writing someone outside your organization or industry . . . someone unlikely to have the slightest idea what the terms mean . . . use everyday words.

Technical terms may impress you, and give you the feeling you really know what you're talking about—but chances are your reader won't have any idea what you mean. And that defeats the purpose of your letter. (It also makes you seem very inconsiderate.)

Be careful using big words—or those with more than one meaning

Remember, the right short words not only make your letter easier to read, they lend an element of precision to your meaning. This precision can be important if you happen to write to a purist who reads for what they mean in the dictionary . . . and not for what common usage has made them mean.

For example: to many people (too many)—"expect" and "anticipate" mean the same thing. In business, for some reason, people never expect anything; they only anticipate things. They should be so lucky.

To expect means to be aware that something probably will happen. To anticipate means to take action before something happens. There's a difference. Now, what if someone wrote this about your impending marriage:

> Mr. Jones and his fiancée anticipate getting married in June.

Even if it's true, it's a mean thing to say in public. The sentence should have read:

> Mr. Jones and his fiancée expect to be married in June.

Try not to use complex, rambling sentences

Don't get caught up in wordy sentences or paragraphs— or those making more than one point at a time. Just assume the attention span of your reader is somewhat limited. It's a safe assumption. He won't make the effort to follow your thought process through endless convolution (wow! we mean endless twisting and turning) before getting to the point.

You know, if John Double said:

> While I was attending our sales meeting on prices for next year's products, my wife stopped off at the dress shop in the lobby of your hotel where she purchased a dress to wear to the dinner for salesmen and their wives after the meeting. Unfortunately, she did not have any credit card with her and gave the hotel registrar as a reference since our meeting was held there. I want you to know I appreciate his doing it for her.

Which twin has the toni . . . or which point is more important, the dress or the sales conference . . . or, who cares? You would be so confused by the end of that paragraph you would probably say "forget it."

But if he'd said:

> Please express my thanks to the registrar of your hotel. Last week, he very kindly gave my wife the reference she needed to buy a dress at the shop in your lobby.

Easy to understand? Of course. It is perfectly clear what the writer had in mind . . . to thank the registrar.

Give some thought to your grammar

Correctness for its own sake isn't the object of the drill . . . merely correctness for the sake of making your letters clear. Gross grammatical errors muddy the waters, and make you look ignorant. Take for example something as simple as a misplaced modifier.

"Are you an old movie fan?" A simple question—but asked of a woman who was a bit sensitive about her age. Her reply. "I've been going to movies for years, but I certainly don't consider myself old." Not only did the question insult her, it failed to get the information it was after. It should have read, "Are you a fan of old movies?" She wasn't.

And have you seen the bank advertisement which reads, "We're saving for our retirement at the _____ Bank." Haven't you always wanted to spend your retirement in a bank?

So, split infinitives, end sentences with prepositions, forget the rules you learned way back when—but make sure the grammar you do use doesn't give your letters meaning you never intended.

Be coherent

Make points one at a time and lead logically to the conclusion. Your letters must take the reader by the hand and lead him through your thoughts to the same conclusion you reach. Don't skip around indiscriminately from one point to another. Think about what you want to say, organize your thoughts and then say only what you want to say in the clearest possible way. In short, make sure your reader knows what kind of "cheese" you offer.

COMPLETENESS

An incomplete letter fails to tell the reader that Swiss cheese has holes in it. Or it offers the reader a box seat at the stadium —and doesn't tell him which stadium or how much. Little things like that can make a very big difference.

If you want to be sure your letters are complete, take a hint from the rules most journalists use: tell the reader who, what, when, where, why and how.

So if you were going to offer those stadium tickets you might have written:

> You can pick up box seats, at the bargain price of $60, for all New York Giants football home games at Yankee Stadium during the next season. They're available now—and what better way to enjoy one of America's most popular sports than by being there in person?

WHO—WHAT—WHERE—WHEN—WHY—and—HOW (It's all there—in one paragraph.)

Complete letters get action

Letters are usually written to get action—or to give information. But a letter fails unless you've told your reader all he needs to know to either act, or make some decision.

Suppose you own a large office furniture company. You're holding a Washington's Birthday sale and you've sent this note to your customers:

> We're having a sale of office furniture on Washington's Birthday. I am sure you will find something of interest to you.
>
> We look forward to your coming in.
>
> > Sincerely,

Why? Why should your reader be interested? You haven't made your letter complete. It hasn't given him enough information to make him decide if he will—or won't. Now—

On February 22, we're holding our annual Washington's Birthday sale of office furniture, here at our main store.

Prices will be slashed, *for that one day,* as much as 40% on some items. For example:
   Desks—Black formica sides, with chrome legs and trim and walnut formica tops . . formerly sold for $350 will sell for $210.

Unbelievable? Why don't you come in and let's prove to you it is a reality.

> > Until February 22—

Interested? Of course. This letter gave the reader the information and motivation to make him do what you want. Again, it's all there—WHO—WHAT—WHERE—WHEN—WHY—and —HOW

Incomplete letters cause more work

If your letter isn't complete, you could be asking for the chore of writing follow-up letters. Many people complain about the number of follow-ups they have to write. They even tend to blame the readers . . . to doubt their intelligence because they haven't answered. But usually the writer brought on the situation in the first place by writing an incomplete letter.

It isn't difficult to do; the most well-meaning people do it. (But not the people who plan their letters!)

As part of its good employer program, a large organization sent this letter to its employees:

Date

To Our Employees:

As a reward for all the effort our employees have put toward the success of our Company, we are pleased to announce a new Share-the-Profit-Plan.

This plan is available to all employees who qualify. All that is necessary is that the employee designate a certain % of his salary each month to be invested in our company stock. In turn, the Company will invest the same % in the employee's name.

For instance: Jim Cash allots 3% of his salary for investment. The Company allots an additional 3%. So that, in effect, Mr. Cash has a total of 6% invested in his name.

This is our way of saying "Thank you" for your loyalty.

Cordially,

President

And then management sat back and waited for the flood of applications from its employees. But they didn't come. Oh, yes, some did—but far from what was expected.

Why? This seems like a pretty good letter, don't you think? You don't? And you're so right.

It's not complete

(1) It tells you there will be such a plan, but doesn't tell *when* it is effective.

(2) It mentions the plan is available to all who qualify, but doesn't tell *how* to qualify.

(3) It says all that is necessary is to designate a per cent of your salary, but it doesn't tell you *how* to make that designation.

(4) It's called a Share-the-Profit-Plan, but doesn't tell you *when* you'll share in that profit.

Sorry. But without the HOW and WHEN of that magical journalists' formula—it isn't complete. And the next step is a follow-up letter from management giving this information in order to get the reply from each employee.

It's just got to be

—WHO

—WHAT

—WHERE

—WHEN

—WHY

and

—HOW

CONCISENESS

Conciseness is simply saying what you have to say in as few words as possible. That doesn't mean be blunt. But it does mean you shouldn't be infatuated with yourself and carry on and on. And on. Redundance and superfluous words are a waste of time . . . yours and your reader's. A concise letter cuts out unnecessary words, but includes everything necessary to get your message across.

Here again, planning before you write or dictate is important. If you have a clear view in your own mind of what you want to say—you're much less apt to wander around trying to say it. And that's good. Wandering around in print gets tedious and tedium doesn't get read.

Nearly every routine situation can be handled in two or three paragraphs. And it's almost never necessary to go beyond one page. Unless you insist on long words and lengthy phrases; beating around the bush; giving unnecessary details; repeating what the reader already knows.

Take long words—

Why use	*When these will do*
Advise	Tell
Aggregate	Total—entire
Collocate	Gather—collect
Communication	Note—letter—wire
Converse	Talk
Document	Paper—form
Forward	Send—mail
Judicatory	Legal
Procedure	Plan—way—system
Tendered	Offered—gave
Terminate	End
Traverse	Travel

Or lengthy phrases—

Instead of	*How about*
during the course of	during
in order to	to
succeed in making	make
with reference to	about
for the purpose of	for or to
along the lines of	like
are of the opinion	believe
as to	about
for the reason that	because
information in our records	our information
if we find it possible	if we can
we would like to ask that you	please
in lieu of	instead
we would appreciate the benefit of	we need
check in the amount of	check for

Remember, the longer your phrases and sentences, the more words you use to say what you want to say—the greater the likelihood you'll lose the reader. Don't risk it. This isn't to say you should be simple . . . just uncomplicated.

Mr. Wordy dictated:

Would you be so kind as to sign your name to the attached authorization and return it to us immediately in the enclosed self-addressed, stamped envelope.

And Miss Brief transcribed:

Please sign the attached authorization and return it immediately in the envelope enclosed.

Let's take a look at the extra words:

	Why not
Would you be so kind	Please
Sign your name	Sign (what but your name?)
Return it to us	Return it (return is to go back to.)
Enclosed, self-addressed, stamped envelope	Enclosed envelope. (He can see it is all the other things.)

26 words vs. 13—50% fewer for the same message!

Weeding out phrases that are unnecessarily long won't automatically shorten your letters. In fact, the length of any message is determined only by what has to be said—and there isn't any arbitrary limit to judge by. If you need twenty-five words, use twenty-five words. If you need fifty pages, use fifty. Just don't waste any of the space you use.

Involved sentences—

As was the case with Clarity, short words and sentences help you get to your point quickly. Long, involved sentences are difficult to read; they generally include several thoughts and the reader must juggle till he sees what you're driving at.

> My head is light with the feeling of indiscretion which makes me sense it would be nice for me to have someone else share my adversities as well as my triumphs, and I have selected you as the leading candidate. An affirmative reply would be appreciated.

Wouldn't it be much easier—and certainly more effective—to simply say, "Will you marry me?"

Using overly long sentences delays getting to the point, and that sort of delay is an invitation to the reader to put your letter aside. Not exactly the reaction one hopes for.

Or blunt sentences—

Naturally, there's a limit to how far you should carry the practice of shortening sentences. There's no rule to follow here . . . just good sense. And one of the traps hiding behind short sentences is that they can be blunt . . . so blunt they put your reader off his feed. It's possible to be too short, too concise. Such letters lack warmth and tact. They make people angry.

In the extreme you'd be insulting almost any reader by writing:

> My name is Mr. Jones. I am answering your letter. We sell chairs. We don't sell the chairs you want. I am sorry.

This is a reversion to "See Dick Run" and the monotony of it would be laughable. Perhaps the solution is to be sure all sentences are as tight as they can be without being ridiculous. If some are long, it's not a disaster . . . in fact, it will add variety to your style. Just avoid being pompous.

COURTESY

In themselves, clarity, conciseness and completeness aren't enough to make a letter successful. A letter can say exactly what you want it to say, say it thoroughly, and say it quickly— and yet you could make an enemy for life.

Once your letter is formed in your mind, and you're at the position where you can begin writing it, make yourself aware of one more thing: *how you say what you say*.

Letters are written, obviously, to accomplish some purpose. The tone of a letter, the words used, the attitude conveyed can completely eliminate any chance of positive accomplishment.

Usually, people don't purposely offend or irritate the person to whom they write. But it's surprising how many letters do offend or irritate. These letters are packed with implications and attitudes the authors wouldn't dream of making in face-to-face conversation. This sad state of affairs is largely due to thoughtlessness and a lack of knowledge of or concern for good human relations.

Just about everyone likes to feel important; most people are self-centered; many people are skeptics. These traits had best be kept in mind. Otherwise, you're apt to annoy people. And people who have been annoyed are the kind who can cause you trouble. What to do about this? Several things.

Put your reader in your letter

The overuse of "I," "we," "company," and similar references is sheer poison to your reader. He'll almost certainly lose interest in what you have to say if he gets the slightest hint you're placing your own interest before his. Like this little gem:

> *We* received your letter of (date) and *we* are looking into the matter. As soon as *we* have had the opportunity to assemble the information from *our* records, *we* will give a full reply.

There's the distinct impression here that the author doesn't give a damn for his reader. "We" used 4 times, and "our" once. The word "you" apparently never came to mind. But look at this:

You asked a good question, Mr. Kimble. And *your* answer will be along in just a few days. The facts *you'll* want aren't all in one spot, but they're being gathered for *you* now.

"You" four times—not a "we" in the message. That kind of response can't possibly irritate your reader. He'll love it!

And the words "company," "company rules," "company policy," are all common blunders. The public couldn't care less about rules and procedures. When you can't do what someone asks because there *is* a rule against it, don't hide behind the rule; explain the situation. Don't slap your reader down with a curt "against our rules and policies." If a person has shown enough interest to write, he deserves a better explanation.

Dear Mr. Dud:

We have your request for a personal loan of $1600. We are sorry to have to turn you down, but our company rules will not permit us to lend you that much money personally.

Yours truly,

Can't you just hear Mr. Dud? "What have I done? You'd think I was a criminal or something! Who do they think they are?"

But with a little explanation on the part of the banker, two things might have happened . . . Mr. Dud wouldn't have been offended—and it might have been possible for him to qualify after all.

We're pleased, Mr. Dud . . .

that you thought of the First Bank when you needed some extra cash. However, we can't lend over $1000 to anyone on just a signature.

But if you can get someone to cosign the papers with you, we'll be more than glad to present your request to our loan committee.

Sincerely,

Forget files and records

As for files and records, it may shock you to know that nobody cares where you keep your information. All they care about is your ability to give them information. Don't mention files and records . . . it makes you sound as if you don't know what you're talking about. Which is no way to inspire confidence in what you say later. If the information is buried in the files, just tell your reader you are gathering the information and you'll send it as soon as you can.

> In looking through our files, we find that there are two installment payments left on your account. As soon as they have been paid, we will be glad to mark our records so that your account can be opened again at any time for new purchases.

The reader doesn't care how you found out there are only two payments left . . . and it doesn't matter whether or not you mark your records. All that matters is:

> Only 2 payments left, Mr. Able, and your account will be all ready for your convenience any time you make a new purchase.

Those are the facts; and you save the reader's time, and sound so much more sincere if you just state them and omit the other references that are of no concern.

Never, never lecture

Some people pull the neat trick of lecturing readers . . . talking down with a disturbingly paternalistic attitude. If you do it, you're better off not writing letters at all. This trait is especially evident in businesses that aren't completely familiar to the man on the street—such as insurance, banking or scientific or technical professions.

These businesses are carried on amid technical, specialized terms that not many outside their own four walls can understand. If those terms are used in letters, the readers are going to be piqued.

But all businesses . . . all letter writers . . . must avoid expressions which go against the reader's grain. People love to read meanings into letters, and it doesn't take much ambition to find the wrong meaning where it was not intended. Aside from using purely technical terms, here are some phrases that make readers bristle!

> As we previously told you
> If you had read my last letter carefully
> You apparently didn't notice
> You should have known
> Your letter is not clear
> You can't expect us
> You are mistaken
> You are being unreasonable
> It should be obvious to you

If it soothes your nerves to *think* those phrases, go ahead. But for Heaven's sake don't let your reader know what you're thinking. If your letters have to accomplish some positive purpose, being negative won't help.

Watch for words that have a bad ring

Many words have meanings, connotations, outside their strict dictionary definition. The same words mean different things to different people. So you'll probably never be entirely sure that some of your words aren't being misconstrued.

But some words have a bad ring to many people. "Execute" is one. Why not "carry out," "implement"? "Delinquent" is a touchy one. Letters don't offer voice inflections and facial expressions to soften the blow of the words. So choose carefully.

Here are some to stay clear of:

> You "failed" or "neglected"
> Your "complaint"
> You "must" or "should"
> We "insist" or "demand"

Try not to forget that the person reading your letter is human, and likes to be treated as such . . . even as you and I.

Leave your reader an "out"

In any controversy, most of us like to prove we're right. Not just partly right, but absolutely right. Crush the other guy! Crush his ego, his pride—maybe even his confidence. Charge! Splat! (That last sound was a friendship caught between two thick heads.)

No one likes to be belittled. No one likes to be made to appear foolish. No one likes to have his opinion, attitudes discounted as worthless. Yet many times a letter attempts to do just that . . . probably an unconscious attempt by the writer to make himself feel more important. The worst offenders are usually the ones who are least sure of themselves . . . like the guy who knows least and shouts loudest in an argument.

Cultivate the habit of letting the other person save face. Don't criticize or question his intelligence, judgment or opinions so that the situation becomes an either/or predicament. Leave the guy an "out." The next time you could be in his shoes.

Try not to contradict anyone openly. It's reasonable to say you have a different point of view, but don't pull the plug all the way out. Never get involved in name-calling. It's a child's game.

Never point a finger at your reader: "you did it, not me." Louis Nizer once said that "the person who points a finger has four fingers pointed at himself."

Don't try to save your own ego at the expense of someone else. If you've made a mistake, admit it and apologize. Alibis are worse than saying nothing.

NOT:

> You said that 60% of all working women are married. You were wrong. I checked with U. S. Labor Statistical Abstract and found it is 62.2%.

BUT THIS:

> We seem to have arrived at different figures for the same fact. You get 60% and I get 62.2%. Shall we try for a third source to see which is correct? My information came from U. S. Labor Statistical Abstract.

NOT:

> When you applied for your loan at this bank, you were asked for all previous lending organizations with which you had dealt in the past 5 years. Now we find you neglected to tell us about the First National loan 3 years ago.

BUT THIS:

> It's not always easy to remember everything 5 years back, and I'm sure that's why the loan at First National wasn't listed in your application to us.

NOT:

> The stock dividend check we mailed you should have been for $20 more. We are, therefore, enclosing an additional check in that amount.

BUT THIS:

> Forgive us for any inconvenience we may have caused by sending you the incorrect stock dividend. It should have been for an additional $20—and it is enclosed.

Letters are a major means of building and holding good will. They are also a major means of bringing about actions that will hopefully benefit companies. Letters that make people dislike you right at the start, and then go on to challenge to a fight—or leave no choice but a fight—don't build good will or result in constructive action. All they can do is hurt you.

Sooner or later, everyone who deals with the public, in person, on the phone or through letters, learns the need to be courteous and respect the rights and feelings of others. It's true the world of business is not a big popularity contest, but getting along with people is essential to success in business. And business holds a franchise with the public only as long as it holds public good will.

Be kind! Be diplomatic! Some situations will give you no choice but to be firm and forceful, but don't go to extremes. Don't charge like a mad bull . . . cool it. Be firm but rational. And in cases where you do have a choice, keep the other person in mind. Never forget, to the other guy you are the other guy.

Reflect

And, once again let's turn back to page 16, Chapter I . . . our friend, Mr. Street. Remember, he was concerned because we had investigated him?

Remembering that the body of our letter must be . . .

Clear

Complete

Concise

Courteous

we wrote:

You see, these are the people who know   (*Right to*
you best—the people who told us how   *the point*)
fine an individual you are.

Since every life insurance company must   (*Complete—all*
protect its insureds and their investment,   *reasons why we*
most of us investigate applicants in ad-   *did it—and*
vance; and eliminate those who are poor   *the result*)
insurance risks. Your application has been
processed . . . and we find you to be a
preferred risk. Our apologies for any con-   (*Courteous and*
cern our inquiry might have caused.   *apologetic.*)

(And we believe everything is clearly stated.)

CLEARNESS—COMPLETENESS—CONCISENESS—COURTESY .

—the major characteristics of the middle of any good letter.

And if each letter you write keeps these in mind you're bound
to get your message across effectively. We can see that mouse's
nose twitching . . . he's on his way . . . so we'll get on to the
ending of our messages and bring that mouse right into our
trap.

4.

At the end

The ending of a letter serves the same purpose as the punch line of a joke.

Unfortunately, the imagination in the endings of most letters is about the same as the imagination of the guy we all know who insists on continually repeating the same joke. And the reaction to those endings is the same . . . at best, ho-hum; at worst, disaster.

But good letters and good endings aren't jokes. It's sad so many of them are laughable. Like the letter that offers no service whatever, and ends, "If we can be of further service . . ." Yet, there is at least one person who won't laugh— the person to whom you're writing. He'll wonder if you're for real—and if you're sane.

Just like the rest of your letter, the ending must be planned. It should follow logically from what has come before. And it should leave the reader with a favorable impression. The ending is the last part of your message the reader sees. Make sure it's remembered. If it isn't, you might as well not have written.

There are two broad categories of endings: those which ask for action of some kind, and those which are designed to leave a certain impression with the reader—but don't require action.

It has been estimated that 60% of the letters written to get action achieve nothing, either because they have weak endings, ungracious endings, or no endings at all. Weak endings are an invitation to delay . . . perhaps your reader thinks you're not serious, or he can put you off with no serious consequences. Whatever his thinking, unless he acts your letter fails. If you want someone to take prompt, specific action, your endings *must tell him:*

►What you want done

►When you want it done.

►How the reader should go about doing it

This can be accomplished without being antagonistic or offensive . . . simply show your reader how he'll benefit from doing as you say. Don't forget, most people like to procrastinate (even if the action is in their own best interest) unless they have a very good reason for acting at once.

Give them the reason—and don't be weak about it. "We remain," "Looking forward to hearing from you," "Thank you for your prompt attention" are all weak endings. On the other hand, "Unless you send us your check immediately, we'll crush you financially" is a bit strong.

Here are some effective closes:

►You'll save money by acting today. And your family will benefit from your thoughtfulness.

►If you place your order no later than March 10, you'll get the advantage of our special rates. Beat the seasonal rush by acting now.

►If you can give us the final figures by this Friday, we will be able to meet your deadline; otherwise, the project will go into overtime.

►Only 10 days remain before your valuable protection will be lost and the security you've built for your family will stop. Send your check, today, for that overdue premium and keep your family's protection in force.

►The furniture will be delivered on Saturday, June 8. Please be sure someone is home to receive it. If this is not convenient, just phone me at 212-3131.

Each of these closings tells:

►What is to be done

►When it should be done

►How it should be done

And remember . . .

Make it sound easy for the reader to act

Letters asking for action are faced with two problems: most people have a tendency toward being lazy—even businessmen and women—and they don't want to work too hard to take the action you want. Also, a busy person may not want to take the time to do what you want. So make it easy—with closes like:

►Just initial the bottom of the letter and return it to me. We'll be on our way.

►All you have to do is check the appropriate box on the return postcard and drop it in the mail.

►Just phone me collect. Your order will be shipped immediately.

►Drop in whenever you're in the area. We'll be proud to show you the largest assortment of desks in the state.

►No check to write—just indicate your willingness to help by initialing the enclosed card. Your contributions will be automatically deducted from your paycheck. And, 50,000 orphans will thank you for your generosity.

Make it hard for the reader to say "No"

There are among us some geniuses who have made millions of dollars by the simple ploy of making it hard for readers to say "no,"—or making the reader take some action to say "no."

The late Nelson Doubleday, Sr., former head of Doubleday & Company, is credited with building book clubs, as we know them, on the premise "make it hard for the customer to say 'no.'"

Don't return this postcard *if you want* the book offered.

And direct mail pieces sell many things on trial . . .

If after 30 days you aren't completely happy, send the radio back and we'll refund your money.

These techniques take advantage of a human tendency to order on impulse and then say "The heck with it. I don't want this. Oh, well, it's only five bucks." And so they don't bother returning it. In effect . . . a sale for the company!

YOU, too, can be a genius. These endings will force your reader to respond to stop an action:

►Unless we hear from you by April 1, we'll assume the order is correct as it stands.

►If I don't get word by the 10th, I'll go ahead.

►The television will be on its way, unless you tell me otherwise before next Tuesday.

►I know you ordered the green-on-blue damask spread, Mrs. Coy, but we no longer have that pattern. Rather than leave you without a spread, however, I have taken the liberty of sending you the blue-on-green. (The colors are identical —just reversed.) And, if you can't use it, just return it.

Then, there are times when all you want to do is—

Shut off further correspondence

Often we have cases where the action to be taken is negative. You want the reader to get off your back . . . stop bugging you . . . and stop writing. This is a more difficult ending, because all too often the person is a valuable customer.

So, this needs delicate and tactful treatment—but at the same time must get the message across.

►I can appreciate your feelings, Mr. Johnson, and I hope you can appreciate mine. We simply can't in good conscience make an exception for you that we won't make for everyone. That would be unfair and would not inspire the confidence all our customers have a right to expect.

►I admire your spirit, Mr. Dunning. And the most pleasant thing for me would be to say "yes." But I hope you see now that it just isn't possible. Sorry to disappoint you, but we will have to stick with our previous decision.

►Contrary to what you may think, we really don't enjoy saying "no" to claimants. But I hope you can see that, even in light of the new information, our answer must still be no.

On the other hand, it's sometimes wise to—

Leave the door ajar

Haven't you been tempted to say "no"—or about to make a firm, categorical decision—and decided it's best not to? At least, it's best not to make the decision firm in a letter. Leave a little leeway.

A good example of how important that can be is the case of young Mr. Carle who visited a large advertising agency looking for a job. Shortly after, he received a letter saying there were no openings for him. Period.

He took another job, and within a few years had risen to a position of some importance. At least that first agency thought so because it approached him about handling their account. When the agency representative walked into Mr. Carle's office, he looked . . . and said, "I remember you. You're the guy who wouldn't hire me." Thus began . . . and ended . . . the interview.

Now don't misunderstand. Of course, you aren't going to hire just anyone. But just because you never know what the future can bring, it's a good idea to cover yourself and leave that door open at least a crack.

This story could have had a different ending if the fellow who wrote that letter had simply closed with something like:

►Unfortunately, at present we don't have any openings on a level suitable to your excellent background and qualifications.

►I'm sorry there isn't anything open at present that would make the best use of your many talents.

►Although at the present, we have nothing in your scope of interest, positions do open from time to time. So keep in touch every once in a while . . . just in case.

Although Mr. Carle might not have been happy with the news, he couldn't have been angry with this treatment.

There are instances, too, when just a little more information, or a different set of circumstances, could change decisions.

►Can you give me any additional facts about this case? If so, we might be able to give it more positive consideration.

►Our present thinking is we won't be able to use your services for about a year. But things happen rapidly around here, so please don't hesitate to check with me from time to time.

►We wish we could pay these medical expenses. But the bills you've submitted do not yet meet your deductible amount. Are you sure you sent all of them? If you do find others, be sure to send them to me at once.

Endings such as these give you a chance to avoid making a final decision until you're absolutely sure you have all the information for a good decision. At the same time, they leave your reader with the impression you're making every effort to be fair.

And, on occasion, it's important to—

Reassure your reader

In business, one of the most difficult tasks is to turn people down, refuse them something they think is their due.

Since these people may be important to your business, whether or not they deserve what they're asking, it isn't wise to flatly turn them down without some reassurance this is not how you want to treat them. Nor what they can always expect.

Perhaps you've made an error—and been caught. (And you can pretty nearly bet next week's paycheck, when you make an error there's always someone to catch it . . . and let you know.) Your letter had better reassure the reader that errors are an exception in your organization.

Endings to fit these situations must be sincere . . . even a little humble . . . or the customer may be lost.

▶I hope you can see this is one of the very few times merchandise cannot be refunded.

▶You have every right to expect and receive excellent service. We will do our best not to let this happen again.

▶Try as we do not to let them, mistakes occasionally get by. But please be sure we will do our best to see none happen with your account again.

▶It is unfortunate this is the only illness your policy does not cover. And, although we hope you won't be taken ill again, if you are, remember you are covered for all other sickness.

Nothing's nicer than to—

Express appreciation

People like to know they're appreciated. They like to be thanked for what they do . . . even if they haven't done much! Whenever you write a letter acknowledging an order, a favor, or to let someone know you appreciate what has been done, the ending is a most effective place to concentrate your message.

▶Thanks for the tip, Joel. You saved me a lot of inconvenience and I'll look forward to returning the favor.

▶Many thanks for thinking of us. It was our pleasure to help, and we hope to have the chance to work with you again.

▶How can I adequately thank you for all you've done! You were so kind at a time when kindness really was important.

▶You did an absolutely perfect job of selecting the furnishings for our new home! Thank you so much . . . and be sure to use me as a reference.

Compliment or congratulate

One of man's greatest weaknesses is his susceptibility to flattery. People love it. They thrive on it. Use it in your endings.

If you're sincere, and the reader knows you're presenting genuine (sounding) flattery, it's about the most effective way to end a letter. And it can be a good way to spur people to goals the company may have set for them.

► In the past you've had a top-notch sales record. I know you'll keep it up in the coming year.

► Your achievement in the past weeks is nothing short of amazing! We're all so proud and look forward to more success for you in the future.

► The work you did was great . . and essential to the success of the entire project. Here's hoping we can work together again soon!

► It's great to see your company recognize you as a very unusual person. Congratulations on your new appointment!

► Landing that million-dollar account is no small achievement. Congratulations, Len!

And there will be those times when endings require—

No action

Since these letters won't have to concentrate on getting your reader to do anything . . . this is a great opportunity just to build good will for your company—and yourself. Say something warm, friendly . . . but the important thing is to say *something*. Don't just end your message without some close.

►I've enjoyed corresponding with you.

►Perhaps we can be helpful another time. I look forward to it.

►Any time you are in the neighborhood, please drop by.

►Thank you for thinking of us.

Now for the more difficult endings—

Apologize and express regret

The proud among us won't like this approach very much. But success in handling people, by letter or in person, means putting your pride in your back pocket. And in business, just as in every part of our lives, there are times when an apology is the only proper solution. Frankly, an apology may be the only way to keep your reader's good will, and business.

Let's make a point right here, though. When you've made an error, we recommend that you admit it at once in the opening of your letter. That's important. Never wait until the closing to make your admission. *But repeat your apology* in the close.

►Thanks for bearing with us while we straightened out the problem we created. As you know, it's the first time, and we'll do everything we can to see that it's the last.

►You've been so patient, Mr. Hanes, while we've been running down our error. We do appreciate it, and most certainly will do everything to prevent anything like it happening again.

►May I say again . . I'm sorry for the inconvenience our error caused.

There are also times when we have to do things—or not do things—that we regret. And an expression of regret at the end of a letter in which you've had to tell someone bad news is a purely human response (as well as good public relations). It leaves the impression that you're a pretty good guy, after all.

►Bill, my friend, we tried . . we really tried. But I'm afraid the answer has to be "no." I'm sorry.

►Those are the rules, Jim. Please understand, I'm not apologizing for them . . they're necessary to run an efficient business. I'm only sorry they prohibit a project which meant so much to both of us.

►I know how hard you worked for this contract, Mr. Adams. I hope you understand why we had to place our order elsewhere. I'm sorry not to bring you better news.

And, of course, there's the—

Personal ending

It's fairly common in business to write letters to people we know well . . . people we've gone out with, whose homes we've visited . . . people we're happy to know and see as individuals, aside from their position as colleagues or contacts in the business world.

When we write such people, it doesn't make sense to be formal, or stiffly "correct" in our letters. Loosen up . . . be natural . . . especially in letters like these. This is a friend you're writing. And the ending is a good place to remind your friend that you think of him as a friend. In the ending— or even with a P.S.—say something that will mean more than the business purpose of the letter.

►Remember me to Kate and the kids. Tell Paul I'll bring that Yankee bat next month when I'm in Cleveland.

►When do you move into that new house? Can't wait to see it.

►Next time you come to town, Sam, bring the family. You and I can visit the boat show while the girls haunt that antique shop they love so much. And the kids can have a ball at the zoo.

Now let's backtrack to our friend, Mr. Street, from Chapter I. We saw how we developed our opening—we worked up our story in the body—and now we need an appropriate close.

Remember the problem? Mr. Street was unhappy about the credit investigation we conducted. After complimenting him right at the start by saying what "an excellent prospect" he was . . . and explaining in the body why the credit investigation was important . . . we're ready—hopefully—to end in a way that sells Mr. Street on accepting the policy.

Before working with this book, the ending on the letter sent Mr. Street might have sounded like—

> We are sure our explanation will help you understand why we conducted a credit investigation about you.

(This should make Mr. Street's blood boil! What right have we to assume, because we explained something, our reader should understand and accept it? In addition, if the letter had been properly written to this point, Mr. Street should have forgotten the unpleasant words "credit investigation." This would just open old wounds—and never sell him the policy.)

Or if we closed with—

> We have issued your policy and it will be delivered by your agent on Monday.

(How presumptuous! Mr. Street originally indicated we could keep the policy if our explanation wasn't darned good. More humility—and hope—on our part would certainly help get him to accept that policy.)

And so we closed with—

> Thanks to your friends, we know you better and look forward to welcoming you as one of our nearly 2 million insureds.

(We complimented him again, by reminding him his friends really thought him great; and we added that quality of hope by "looking forward to welcoming him"—not flatly saying "we welcome" which would assume too much; and we sold the company just a bit more by impressing him with its size— "nearly 2 million insureds."

Simple? Of course . . . because we planned our letter through.

One last thought—

Put sell in your endings

You may have noticed by now that every ending is a form of salesmanship . . . whether you sell confidence in your company, yourself, your judgment, your decision.

Whichever ending you use, it has the secondary objective of selling something, as well as the primary objective of stating a position. Remember that endings are at least as important as the other parts of the letter. They're like the punch line of jokes . . . without them, no matter how good the story that comes before, a bad or inappropriate punch line kills the whole thing.

So, think your endings through carefully. Make the most of them!

5.

Words--plain and simple

Most people don't think about vocabulary . . . don't even know that each person actually has three vocabularies: one for the office, one when he's out with the boys and one for the wife and kids . . . just kidding. The three are:

▶ a reading vocabulary, the largest of the three

▶ a writing vocabulary, about two-thirds the size of the first

▶ a speaking vocabulary, about 60% the size of the first

The ability to learn and use new words probably never leaves us if that ability is cultivated, but the fact is that most people stop learning new words around the age of twenty-five. For people in business, that's bad timing. Most of a successful person's involvement in business . . . exposure to increasingly complex and sophisticated concepts . . . will come after the age of twenty-five. And that person will find it necessary to express thoughts related to those concepts.

But thoughts aren't confined to just a few words, and certainly not solely to the words learned years ago. To express yourself best, you simply can't afford to restrict yourself to the same words in all your letters.

There's probably no end of reasons why we stop learning new and better ways of expressing ourselves. Habit may well be one of the major reasons . . . the habit of always using certain words and phrases we like a lot and being too lazy to learn more. If your letters are ever going to be as good as they can be, as good as they have to be to achieve what you want of them, the habit has to be broken.

Think back. How many letters have you read in the past few months which have really stirred you—made a strong, favorable, lasting impression? How many have you written that were especially effective?

Have you analyzed the good ones to see what made them good? The reasons are the same as the reasons we find some people interesting and fun to be with—while others are bores. Good letters have personality . . . they sound as if they were being spoken by the person who wrote them.

Whether or not you admit it, every letter reflects your personality, and the reader will judge what he reads, even if your true personality doesn't show through. On the basis of your letters people might be judging you to be a fool, or a bore—or even worse, an incompetent with no feel for people and no personality worth talking about. If these judgments are, in fact, true, you're in trouble. Big trouble. But if they can be corrected by getting your true personality into your letters, make every effort to correct them.

How? It's simple.

Get rid of pet phrases

Nothing destroys a potentially good letter faster than phrases that are automatic—obviously stock, requiring no thought. Dick Morris used to give this example:

A man explains to his wife the results of his visit to the butcher: "This is to acknowledge, dear, that I contacted the butcher as per your request. In view of the fact that he did not appear to have the lamb chops on hand that you specified, he advised me to advise you that he will forward same to you under separate cover at an early date."

No one in his right mind would use that language to tell his wife he couldn't get the lamb chops. (Or if he did—bachelorhood, here he comes!) But most people would use that language in a business letter. Why? Business people are as impressionable as wives . . . they can think, just as easily as your wife, that you're crazy; maybe more easily. Canned phrases simply don't do justice to your letters—and certainly don't do you justice! Here are some to avoid. Force yourself!

Phrases to Drop	*We Suggest*
According to our records	"We find"
At the present time	"Now"
At an early date	Give the date—be specific
Be in a position to	"Can"—"Able"
Due to the fact that	"Because"—"Since"—"As"
Enclosed you will find	"Here is" (Don't make him hunt)
Checked our records	"Checked" (Doesn't matter what)
For your information	Omit—it's obvious
In accordance with	"As"
In the amount of	"For"
In order that	"So"
It is our opinion	"We feel"
Send it to my attention	"Send it to me"
Our files indicate	"We find"
We do not appear to have received	"We did not receive." (Stop hedging)
We direct your attention to	"You'll notice"
We are not in a position to	"We can't"
We are in receipt of	"We have"

All these phrases are as old as the hills. If you still use them, they tell people you don't think much about what you say.

Use up-to-the-minute expressions

Advertising, publicity, radio and television are all great sources for words and phrases which are expressive—and timely. When a particular group of words hits the country—make use of them. It shows you are up on things. Use them while they're popular—but drop them once they begin to die out. Remember—you want to be right up on things!

For example:

"Would you believe"

You can do all kinds of things with this.

   "Would you believe $20? $15? Maybe $10?"

A great way to begin a letter putting a price on something you have for sale.

"Piece of the action"

Perhaps not as dignified as you might need on some occasions —but so expressive when written to the right person.

   "We now have 350 new customers, Bill, and Joe would like
   a piece of the action."

Much more interesting—and timely—than to simply say that Joe wants to become a partner.

"Togetherness"

So expressive if you're talking about families, homes, activities.

"The Blahs"

Alka Seltzer made this famous—but can't you picture yourself writing to someone early on Monday morning; not really with it yet; and simply excusing yourself 'cause you've got "The Blahs?" How great!

There are lots of these phrases . . . and more coined every day. Listen for them—and try them. You'll find it can become a game just fitting them into your messages. And they can turn an otherwise "just plain letter" into something your reader will thoroughly enjoy.

So, find new ways to say old things. Make a list of ten or twelve expressions you use. Now, think up two or three new ways of saying the same old tired things. Work at it until you have them. Be original. Put sparkle and personality into your letters. Dare to be different—it pays.

Here are a few to get you started. See how many more you can add.

Old: You are right. I made a mistake in figuring.
NEW: I give up. I sure did mess up those figures.

Old: You received a carbon of my memo.
NEW: You were "carboned in."

Old: You can pay it off in easy installments.
NEW: You can pay it off in painless degrees.

Old: Thank you for clarifying my thoughts.
NEW: Thanks for defuzzing my mind.

Old: You may call us collect.
NEW: Be our guest—call collect.

Old: Our hands are tied by the provisions of the contract.
NEW: We're shackled by provisions.

Old: I have the file until the problem is resolved.
NEW: I shortstopped the file until we have the answer.

Old: Hope this date fits into your schedule.
NEW: Hope this meshes with your schedule.

WORDS—PLAIN AND SIMPLE—BUT INTERESTING!

Use action words—not passive

The difference between the two is as between the living and the dead. Words have more than literal meanings—used properly they can persuade, please, pacify, create confidence and induce action. Used improperly they will inspire a ho-hum.

"The market hit the top today." gives you the true feeling of just what happened. Whereas,

"The market rose today." doesn't really make you feel half as excited.

"Glenn wined and dined Grace last night." makes you jealous of the kind of time Grace had. But,

"Glenn took Grace to dinner last night." sounds like a pretty dull affair.

"Johnny whacked the ball over 300 feet." lets you know that ball was hit. Yet,

"Johnny hit the ball over 300 feet." doesn't give the same feeling.

Words are more than letters on a page. They are stories—pictures—thoughts—and those who learn to use them best tell the best stories, present the clearest pictures, express the finest thoughts.

You can be one of those persons!

6.

Credit--that thing the world revolves around

The credit department of any business is one of the most important—and probably one of the busiest. It's also one which usually feels it's been stuck with the meanest tasks . . . gathering information about people's finances and sometimes having to turn them down.

Actually this department has an enormous influence on the success of the organization since it usually decides who will and will not be able to do business on credit.

Precisely for this reason, letters written by the credit department need finesse . . . tact . . . and can't afford to be cold, unfriendly or stuffy. Bad news gets around fast, and if your letters irritate someone whose business you don't want, he may tell a friend whose business you do want. And you lose. Then again, the individual or company you offend today may be a very desirable customer tomorrow. If you've offended, he'll go elsewhere.

That's your challenge if you write credit letters. And if you accept it, remember being a diplomat is a requisite for this job. Patience—perception—persuasiveness all count, too. (And strong nerves are a "must"!)

People the world over are funny, and the world of credit is no exception. It can bring out the best, and it can bring out the worst. One thing you can be sure of—it will bring out something!

Generally, there are four types of credit applicants:

►Those who pay everything promptly and know exactly where they stand financially. And these folk are willing to tell you all.

(Customers in this category give you no trouble at all when you ask for information . . . provided you are considerate and courteous.)

►Those who've given information in the past and had their confidence betrayed. They may be a little shaky about what they tell.

(If they appear to try to hide something . . . they are. But only because they've learned not to trust people. Here you really will need to be tactful—and most sincere.)

►Those who are hiding something because they aren't very proud of their financial position. They aren't afraid of being betrayed . . . they're afraid of betraying themselves.

(These are the most difficult to get information from. But don't be too quick to write them off as not worth the trouble. All of us remember times we were short of cash, so be understanding in your letters.)

►And then there are people who don't know where they stand financially—something like wives who never have the vaguest notion where they stand.

(They might strike you as being like the woman who said to her banker, "What do you mean I overdrew my account? How can I be out of cash when I have all these blank checks left?"

(In such cases, all you can do is be patient and keep digging for the information you want. Your patience will gain you customers . . . and good will.)

Let's look at a few letters of the type you'll need to write before Mr. and Mrs. Buyit become credit customers.

The prospective customer has applied for credit. Now you are . . .

Requesting credit information

Nothing would please us more, Mrs. Miller . .

than to add your name to our growing list of customers who enjoy all our charge privileges.

Would you just take a few moments and fill in the attached statement so we can put the wheels in motion? We're anxious for you to have your credit card just as soon as possible.

                    Thank you for your interest,

As a business man you know, Mr. Verna . .

that everyone does a little checking before issuing charge accounts to new customers. And that's why we're sure you won't mind giving the information asked on the attached statement.

We're looking forward to providing you with any medical supplies you need. And the minute we receive your reply, we'll get right to work opening your account.

                    Thank you so much,

Dear Mr. James:

We're delighted you think enough of Werner's Department store to ask for credit privileges.

Enclosed is a brief form which we ask all new charge customers to fill in. Just as soon as we receive it back, your application will be rushed through—and your account opened.

Again, thanks for thinking of Werner's.

Cordially,

Dear Mrs. Crolus:

One of our great prides is our impressive list of charge-account customers. And we're most flattered to have you want to add your name to that list.

When you have a minute, please fill in the enclosed form . . sign it . . and return it to me. That's all it takes to put us to work at opening your account.

Sincerely,

Often a customer will send an order . . . and at the same time ask to open an account . . .

We are delighted, Mr. Cash . . .

to receive your order. The selection you made is from the finest line we carry.

The desk and cabinet will be ready for you in about 4 weeks. And since you have asked us to put the order in a credit account, that gives us plenty of time to get the usual, routine financial information out of the way. Would you just take a minute, please, and fill out the attached statement?

Thanks so much, and you may be sure any information you give us will be confidential.

Appreciatively,

Perhaps after you wrote, a customer returned the statement . . . but had not filled it all in—omitted the names of other companies which carry her accounts. Don't act as though she did this deliberately—give the customer the benefit of every doubt—write something like . . .

Just one more item, Mrs. Schultz . . .

and we can act on your charge account. Apparently you overlooked question 6 on your statement. And we do need that information before we can issue your credit card.

Won't you fill it in right away, and return it to me in the enclosed envelope?

Thanks very much,

or you might write . . .

12 down and 1 to go, Mrs. Schultz . . .

the statement you returned had 12 questions completed, but apparently question 6 was missed.

Will you please fill it in right away and send it to me? We're anxious for you to have your credit card as soon as possible.

Thanks,

or . . .

May I have your autograph, Mrs. Curley?

The information you returned to me is complete, with one exception. You overlooked that little line on the bottom where your autograph goes.

If you'd take a moment to sign the form and return it in the enclosed envelope, we'll get right to work on opening your account.

Many thanks,

Just remember . . . we want these customers—we need them —so put on your best smile when you dictate letters to them. Make your gladness shine through your letters, and you'll be off to a great start.

All the information is in—you've made your decision. To be or not to be—a customer. We'll begin with the pleasant part.

To be a customer—or—granting credit

Telling a person "yes" is easy . . . it's fun . . . it's painless. We can all do it. For instance:

It's our pleasure, Mrs. Curry . . .

to welcome you as one of our more than 5000 charge account customers. We certainly will do our best to give you the finest merchandise, at the best prices.

Here is your credit card, and we would appreciate it if you would carry it with you any time you visit the store. It will assure you of proper charges and credits to your account.

Welcome,

Beginning May 1, Mr. Kelly . . .

your charge account will be open for anything you care to purchase from our shop. And, frankly, you couldn't have opened it at a better time.

Our annual furniture sale begins May 1, and at this time all sale merchandise is reduced an additional 10% *for charge account customers only*. We hope to see you then, so you may take advantage of this real opportunity.

Welcome,

Everything's in order, Mr. Cash . .

and we appreciate all your help in giving us the information.

Your desk and cabinet left our warehouse yesterday, and you should have them on Saturday. Enjoy them. And, of course, if you have any questions, just give me a ring.

Thanks again,

Of course, there may be other things you'd like to say to your new-found customers . . . and by all means include them. We're giving you only the flavor of your letters—the tone—the style.

Not to be—or—the turndown

Unfortunately, there'll be cases where you have to turn down credit or limit credit. These are the unpleasant parts of the credit man's job. Yet this is the really challenging part.

When you are about to write a letter to a person you must refuse or limit, ask yourself a couple of questions:

►Is his financial position making him a bad risk permanently —or temporarily? (Perhaps it's caused by unusual circumstances which will be corrected soon.)

►Is there any way at all to grant credit without undue risk of the company losing money?

If you come up with the answer that he's a permanent bad risk—and you might be risking company funds—then ask yourself, "What is the most diplomatic way to say 'no'? How would I say it if he were a good friend?"

Then try something like this:

Dear Mr. Smoke:

The most difficult part of a credit manager's job is telling people he can't offer them credit. But one of the more pleasant sides is suggesting it may only be temporary.

I hope that is your situation, and although we must say "no" now, the story will change later. We had really looked forward to having you as a charge customer.

Perhaps later on your own financial picture will look better and additional credit accounts will not be a burden. At that time, won't you please give us another opportunity to consider your account?

Sincerely,

Dear Mrs. Cass:

Nothing would have pleased us more than to welcome you as a charge account customer. Saying "we can't" is difficult.

But from the information we have gathered it would seem wiser, at this time, if you were to make only cash purchases. Perhaps, later, we can take another look at the picture and, hopefully, say "yes."

I'm sorry this had to be our decision. If there is any other way I can be helpful, however, please let me know.

Cordially,

The last thing I want to do, Mr. Wire . .

is turn down your request for credit. After all, we're in business to sell our products . . and charge customers are the best customers.

But unless a charge account can be helpful to a customer—and not a liability—it would be unfair of us to tempt him to use it. And after looking over the information we've gathered, we really do not feel now is a good time to start your account.

But, Mr. Wire, things are bound to improve . . and perhaps then you'll let us take another look—and hopefully be able to open your account.

Until then . .

Dear Mr. Lanis:

The part of my job I like most is saying "yes" to people. The part I like least is saying "no." And unfortunately, this letter is to say right now we can't accept your application for credit.

There is, though, a glimmer of light.

I notice on your application that the great bulk of your financial obligations will be paid up in 6 months. Perhaps it will temper the disappointment you must feel now by suggesting we get together for a chat in 5 months. If things go as you've indicated they will, there should be no question of your being granted full credit privileges at that time.

I wish our good news could be immediate . . but please give us the opportunity to say "yes" 5 months from now.

Cordially,

Why, you may ask, do we include this hope for the future? Most everything in life is built on hope . . . and often just the confidence someone may have in you to make that hope reality will do the trick.

Sometimes we feel we'd rather not say "no," but we're not ready either to give a 100% "yes." You might like to offer credit . . . but on a limited amount.

Thank you so much, Mr. Partial . . .

for thinking of our company when you needed new art supplies. We hope it's the beginning of a long relationship.

You asked us to set up a charge account. That's great! We'll be glad to do it. May we suggest, however, that for the first six months, the credit be limited to $125 monthly? We've made this a practice with all new accounts. Customers like it, because it gives them a chance to evaluate our services and products before committing themselves to heavy credit; we like it, too, because it gives us a chance to get better acquainted with new clients.

After six months, we'll be glad to consider increasing your credit . . and, hopefully, by the end of a year have no restrictions at all.

I sincerely hope this is satisfactory. If I don't hear from you by the end of next week, I'll assume it is, and open your account on this basis.

And, Mr. Partial, every good wish for much success with your studio.

Cordially,

At times, Mr. Weaver . .

being a credit manager reminds me a little of my association with a young lady in college. She's my wife now, but back on our first date when I wanted to kiss her all she'd sit still for was holding hands.

Now I'm in the position of backing off and saying, "For the time being, let's just hold hands." We've reviewed your application for credit, and you've got it . . but with a limit of $1000. I know this isn't as much as you wanted, but in view of your other obligations, it's the best we can offer right now.

As the pressure of your other commitments eases, be sure to let us know. I'm sure we can grant you greater credit limits then.

Sincerely,

Actually, this works to the good of the customer as well as the seller. It keeps the customer of a new business from over-extending himself . . . and that can be helpful in the beginning stages.

Extending credit

Any company which offers charge accounts, or extends credit, is faced at some point with customers who ask for extensions—want a higher limit or more time to pay.

Happily, many times we can give them what they want— they've been good customers and had good reason for asking. When you're able to do as they ask—be nice about it. Not paternalistic and condescending. Just nice.

You might say:

You're right, Mr. Daly . .

We do understand. And we would be glad to give you more time to clear the $112 balance.

As you suggested, we will look for payment of $50 each in mid-June and mid-July, and $12 on August 1.

Glad we could help.

or

We're so sorry, Mr. Paine . . .

about the illness in your family. Of course, we will be glad to give you the extension.

You may take whichever way is most helpful to clear the balance, either—

▶send $50 a month for the next 6 months, or

▶pay the entire balance at the end of the 6 months . . June 30.

Thank you for explaining to us. And we do hope everything comes along well.

Most sincerely,

Unhappily, there will be times when you can't give a customer what he asks. If you can't help him completely, perhaps you can offer a counterproposal—cosigner, or collateral. For example:

We'd like to help, Mr. Time . . .

but we can't extend your credit account any further. When you last asked, you were sure it would help you through a difficult time. But we anticipated that extension was all you would need.

May I offer an alternative? Is there someone who would be willing to cosign for payment of the $300 by a certain date? Under that condition, we might be able to move the final payment date to August 18.

Why not look into that possibility . . and let me have your decision by next Friday?

Sincerely,

REMEMBER . . . PATIENCE—PERCEPTION—PERSUASIVENESS

The credit man's trademark.

7.

Letters that get what you've got coming

Cash flow is mighty important to most companies . . . especially small ones. When a significant number of customers get behind in payments, the pinch can be severe. So, collection letters have a very important role.

Actually, they have two roles . . . keeping the money coming in, and doing it without antagonizing the customer!

Remember—if a customer has fallen behind in payments to you, he is probably in arrears with others also. This means your collection letters will compete with others. Who gets paid first? That depends . . .

.. how badly the customer needs what you offer

.. whether you can offer better terms for settling what he owes

.. what his opinion is of your company, and your attitude toward him.

Usually, the company paid first is the company that shows the most consideration, sincerity and understanding. How do you impress your customer with how much you care? Through your collection letters . . . so they better be good!

COMMON FAULTS IN COLLECTION LETTERS

Too Long—In an effort to bend over backward, and be your customer's best pal, don't get carried away and ramble on and on and on:

Dear Mr. Pabehind:

I'm sure it is an oversight on your part, but there is still an amount outstanding on your loan with our bank. We don't want to seem unfair, but we really do feel you should send us your check now so that we can mark our records closed and we won't have to bother you again with a letter reminding you of this unpaid item.

You will recall you took the loan out with us in January of last year and it was to be repaid in 12 monthly installments of $50 each. You have been very good about paying each month on time—except for this last payment which is now 3 weeks overdue and should be sent to us at once. Won't you please send us your check right away so we can mark our records closed and put your credit rating back in excellent standing?

Sincerely,

Too Short—The other extreme is being curt. Brevity is not, in itself, a fault. If your letters are short, be sure they contain sufficient detail and explanation so the reader can identify what you're saying.

Dear Mr. Pabehind:

Your check for $50 is now 3 weeks overdue. It is the last payment on your loan, and must be made at once. We will expect payment by return mail.

Sincerely,

There is a happy medium—something like:

Have you forgotten, Mr. Pabehind . . .

that last payment on your loan? It's only $50 (and after all you have paid over the year, this amount must seem small). But, it is needed to clear your account.

You've been so prompt all along that I was sure you'd appreciate this little reminder. Won't you just put your check in the enclosed envelope and send it to me today?

Thank you,

NOT TOO LONG . . . NOT TOO SHORT . . . JUST RIGHT

Poor Choice of Words—Collection letters are touchy. Watch your words carefully. You'll have plenty of opportunity to test your vocabulary when you're writing people about the cash they owe.

Like the plague, avoid:

►delinquent

►settlement

►neglected

►claimed

►indebtedness

►direct you to pay

►you stated

►we cannot honor

►submit

Keep in mind what we said in our chapter on Words. They are the key to your thinking. (And the words above are dead giveaways as to what *you're* thinking!)

Inconsistent—Collection letters often overstate the store's patience with customers—and then browbeat the customer in the next paragraph.

Dear Mr. Samuals:

As you know, our policy is to give every customer the greatest possible chance to make suitable arrangements with us for the payment of his bills.

In fact, at the time your account was opened, we went to considerable pains to offer you various payment options, and every year we remind each customer that several modes of payment are available. You were last notified of these options just three months ago, and you, yourself, chose your present mode.

We are, therefore, disappointed that you have not kept your part of our agreement. In view of this, we must ask that your account be paid in full within the week, or we will be forced to turn the matter over to our lawyers for prosecution.

Needless to say, if payment is not forthcoming, we will permanently revoke your charge privileges with us. We would, of course, prefer to spare you this inconvenience and we hope it will not be necessary.

Cordially,

Or sometimes we use threats—and then don't follow them. In some instances customers have been threatened with a lawsuit in a series of letters over a long period. After a while the customer just laughs at what he now knows is just a hollow threat.

When you say, "If we don't hear from you by *April 10,* we will have no choice but to give your account to our attorneys" mean it. And doggone, on April 11 write and tell him, "Your account was turned over to our attorney this morning. I am very sorry this was necessary."

But when you say it—mean it. Or the laugh will be on you.

PLUSSES IN COLLECTION LETTERS

Recognize reasons for not paying—Remember that there are definite circumstances which cause people to forget to pay.

►Lack of cash

►Just plain forgot

►Unhappy with product

►One of those "never on timers"

Keep these in mind, and it will help with the tack your letter takes.

Know your objective—Is it to get the cash and keep the customer? . . . get the cash and get rid of the dead-beat? . . . get the cash before any other debtors do?

Keep your cool—Never let temper show, nor disappointment, nor rudeness. Always be calm, cool—and collect.

Adopt the YOU approach—Keep Mr. Customer's viewpoint in focus. Remember . . . basically, everyone is honest. There's generally a darned good reason why he hasn't paid.

Be sincere—Always be frank. Don't use obvious "excuses" for any action you need to take.

Put yourself in other fellow's shoes—If you do, you'll write the most action-getting, cash-collecting letters of the century.

EFFECTIVE COLLECTION LETTERS

Collection letters come in all sizes and formats . . .

►Printed or typed

►Long or short

►Dictated and tailored to a particular case

►Part of a printed series

►Prepared on a computer

Printed reminder notices

When an account is overdue only a short time, the customer might simply have forgotten. Or, perhaps a temporary squeeze on available cash meant that he had to put your bill off for a bit. (You know—it's happened to all of us.)

And in these cases, a short printed reminder that money is due is enough to get most people to pay. In fact, you might set up a series of two or three—each a little stronger.

Printed notices have several advantages:

(1) cost less,
(2) faster than writing letters, and
(3) look routine and imply the customer is not alone in his plight.

And really, at this early stage a long plea for payment is premature. Just simple stories, like:

(*Reminder No. 1*)

It isn't much . . .

just the small amount shown below. But it is keeping us from marking your account PAID. Won't you put your check in the mail right away?

Thanks so much,

Amount $_____

or

Time passes all too quickly . . .

even the time when payments on our charge accounts are due. By now we had hoped to receive your check for last month's statement.

Before another day passes, please but your check in the enclosed envelope and send it to me.

Thank you,

Amount $_____

(*Reminder No. 2*)

Could the mail be our problem . . .

and the reason we haven't yet received your check for this amount still open in your account? Did you mail the check— but it never reached me?

If so, please put an immediate stop-payment on it and send us a duplicate. We're anxious to mark your account PAID IN FULL.

Concerned,

Amount $_____

or

Something must be wrong . . .

because we've never received your reply to my previous reminder about this open bill. And, since I'm sure you'd like to clear this balance at once, this note is to let you know the amount below is still unpaid.

May I have your check in the next 5 days, please?

Thanks so much,

Amount $_____

(Reminder No. 3)

It's difficult to understand . . .

why the balance in your account is still not paid. Are you unhappy with the merchandise? Did we in some way offend you or fall down on our service?

If so, please let me know at once so we can correct the situation. Otherwise—won't you put your check in the mail immediately, so we can still keep you on our preferred credit list?

Hopefully,

Amount $_____

or

There must be a reason . . .

when an excellent charge account customer like you doesn't pay a bill.

Won't you let me know at once what is keeping your account unpaid? And, of course, if it's just been overlooked, won't you send your check to me immediately so we can continue to consider you an excellent customer.

Thank you,

Amount $_____

A suggestion—

If you use these short, printed messages, it's wise to have a couple or three versions of each. Some people are habitually late . . . and sending the same notice each time will lose its punch.

And a few words of caution—

►Never send more than 3 printed notices.

(If you haven't been successful with 3, you have a serious credit problem requiring your personal attention.)

►Always enclose these messages in envelopes.

(They are confidential and must be treated as such.)

►Use only first-class mail.

(If there's no sense of urgency in your mail, there won't be any in his!)

►Double-check to be certain the check hasn't arrived—before you mail any reminder.

Personal, follow-up collection letters

Printed reminder notices will work in most cases, but there will be others—15% or 20%—where stronger action will be needed. This action is best delivered in personal letters.

They must be forceful, but not rude; explicit, without talking down; attention-getting—but not insincere. And you, the author, will need to use more courtesy, more tact, and have broader shoulders than any other letter writers.

Your letters must:

Give the reader the benefit of the doubt

Perhaps our reminders have been misplaced . . .

We may not have recorded your check when it arrived. Would you please send me a copy of the canceled check, so we may properly credit your account.

With a busy schedule like yours, Doctor, I can understand how you may not have time for your bookkeeping.

Give him an "out"

Have you been trying to phone me about your open account? If so, I can understand why I haven't heard from you—my phone seems tied up all day long.

I know you wouldn't purposely ignore my letters, so there must be another reason why I haven't heard from you about your unpaid bill.

Perhaps you didn't know that we're actually a pretty understanding bunch . . . and if there is some reason why it's difficult for you to pay your bill now, we might be able to make it easier.

Give him an inducement to pay

(1) Appeal to pride—

No one likes to have a poor credit rating.

(2) Appeal to fairness—

You've had the toaster home for several weeks, Mrs. Joe.

(3) Show cooperation—

We'll be more than happy to meet you halfway.

(4) Propose plan of payment—

You may not find it convenient to pay all $75.48 at once. So we suggest—

June 15—$25

July 15— 25

Aug. 15— 25.48

(5) Show benefit—

If you mail your check today, your account will be cleared in time for our White Sale.

(6) Point out possible inconvenience—

It's almost time for Christmas shopping. We'd hate to have you inconvenienced at that time. But unless your present balance has been cleared, we will have no choice but to close your account.

(7) Give alternatives—

You can send the entire $150 by next Wednesday; or send $75 on Wednesday, and the additional $75 ten days later.

(8) Make it sound easy—

Just get your checkbook, pick up your pen, fill out the check for $32, mail it in the enclosed envelope—and your account will be up to date.

(9) Remind of the ultimate consequence—

I'm sure you realize that unless your account is brought up-to-date within the next 7 days, we have no choice but to turn to our attorneys.

Give him a sense of urgency

Time is running out. We must have your check for $123.44 no later than January 3.

Unless I hear from you by August 17, you leave me no choice but to turn your account over to our attorneys.

Only 10 days left, Mr. Flo, in which to clear the balance outstanding on your account. Otherwise, we won't be able to ship the new machines you've ordered.

Now let's take a look at some collection letters which really did the trick . . . and notice the number of "must" points in each.

Are you aware, Mr. Dawson . . .

that *you may be in danger of losing your valuable business credit rating?* Frankly, we would not like to see this happen. *(Appeal to pride)*

Yet, unless we receive your check for this outstanding bill of $409.25 by April 20, *we have no choice but to turn your account over to our lawyers.* I am sure you would agree, *11 months is a long time for a bill to remain unpaid . . unless the merchandise was faulty.* But since we haven't heard from you to that effect, we must assume it is satisfactory. *(Ultimate consequence)* *(Appeal to fairness)* *(Leaving an "out")*

As you know, we have written before— and although we dislike causing you any problem, this must be our last reminder.

Our return envelope is enclosed. Why not make out a check for $409.25, and mail it immediately so it reaches me by April 20? *It will only take a minute* and could save you much trouble and embarrassment. *(Make it sound easy)*

Thank you . . .

Five inducements in one letter!

Nearly everyone has money problems at one time or another . . . even medical people. This is how one firm handled a doctor's request for an extension of time because he had unexpected financial problems. (Notice the clever terminology!)

I was sorry, Dr. Blackstone . . .

to hear of your financial illness. But the prognosis is good and *we have added 90 days to the life of your account.* (*Show cooperation*)

You understand, I'm sure, this is an exception. But you were frank—and your letter was a large plus in your favor.

Two payments, 45 days apart, can take care of your balance. This will clear the $679.75 and heal your credit rating. (*Propose plan of payment*)

Glad we could help . . .

P.S. Don't forget! Your payments of $339.88 and $339.87 must be here on August 10 and September 10! (*Stress urgency*)

Three inducements in one letter—and a lot of understanding. And how about this?

Dear Mr. Parker:

Let's help each other clear your overdue account of $103.83. I'll pay the postage, and you make out the check. (*Show cooperation*)

Invoice ⅌15–44277, June 19, 1967 for $95.50, and invoice ⅌10–0955, February 9, 1968 for $8.33 are not paid.

It's probably just an oversight, and your check for $103.83 will take care of it. (*Give him an "out"*)

I'll look for it *by return mail.* (*Stress urgency*)

Thanks so much . . .

P.S. Here's that postage-paid envelope. (*Make it easy*)

Wouldn't you send your check?

Here's a real show of skill when it comes to collecting money. The company made the mistake in what it charged . . . and five years later we're trying to collect. AND IT WORKS!

1962 was a good year, Mr. James . . .

. . . the year you increased your life insurance coverage.

1963 was a good year, too . . . but . . .

. . . the year we forgot to increase your annual premium by the $50 we told you this coverage would cost.

What does this mean?

(1) Your coverage did increase to $10,000 in 1962.
(2) We would have paid your beneficiary that amount in the event of your death.
(3) The annual premium of $108.49 should have changed to $158.49 in 1963.
(4) Premiums 1963 through 1967 were each short $50.
(5) The total shortage is $250.
(6) We're embarrassed.

I know unexpected bills can cause all of us problems, and we'd like to make payment as convenient for you as possible. As a suggestion, installments of $50 each could be made on the 15th of the month from August through December. Just by putting your checks in the enclosed notices.

Will that method of payment be agreeable with you? Will you let me know by the 20th of this month?

Mr. James, we've been happy to carry this increased coverage for these five years, and I feel sure you will want to put everything in order.

Forgive us,

P.S. Of course, in the future, your annual payments will include the additional $50—or $158.49.

This letter to a patient brought immediate payment to the doctor. Small wonder . . .

How is Susan, Mrs. Kay?

So often new babies bring such excitement and confusion to a home that many other important things get sort of put aside. Perhaps one of those "important things" is the balance of your bill for Dr. Kind's services when she was born. It's $125.

By now your life must be getting back to normal routine and you're beginning to catch up with all the other undone things. I'm sure you were planning to mail a check to the doctor very shortly. May I expect it by July 30?

An envelope is enclosed for your convenience.

Thank you . . .
Pat Herman, R.N.

And for patients with large bills, long overdue, this was a most effective solution:

I'm sure, Mrs. Robertson . . .

that you're as concerned as we are about the $235 still due the doctor for your operation 6 months ago.

And we can understand that often problems arise which make paying obligations difficult. Possibly that is why you haven't paid this bill.

So, may I suggest you pay just part each month for the next 4 months?

July	20—	$58
Aug.	20—	58
Sept.	20—	58
Oct.	20—	61
Total		$235

Unless I hear from you before July 12, I will assume this repayment plan is acceptable to you and will expect your first check for $58. And please don't hesitate to call me if you have any questions.

> Thank you,
>
> Pat Herman, R.N.

Here's a series you ought to enjoy . . . and our thanks to Lou Kriloff, author of *Letterpower in Action* . . .

Please don't throw me in the basket, Mr. Kay . . .

I'm valuable to you. $61.25 sent back to me will revive your perishing credit rating and keep that mean old man with the black mustache from your door.

And here was the answer . . .

Gentlemen:

We received your letter and would like you to know that we are dividing our creditors into three groups:

1. Those who will be paid promptly
2. Those who will be paid sometime
3. Those who will never be paid

You will be happy to know that due to the friendly tone of your letter, we have promoted you from group three to group two!

Need we say more?

Discount . . . "If paid within 10 days—"

If your business offers discounts to customers who pay within, say, five or ten days, chances are you'll run into people who discount too much—or take discounts they're not entitled to.

Usually they've just made an honest mistake . . . a misunderstanding . . . and the situation can be set right with a polite letter explaining the story.

Yet, occasionally, you'll have an out-and-out phony trying to get away with a discount he knows he doesn't deserve—hoping not to be caught. If he happens to you . . . bite your tongue and be polite with him, too.

If you write a nasty letter complaining about the situation, it could go to someone who didn't know anything was wrong. (Frequently, for example, a clerk tries to be cute, or make himself look good.) But, based on your nasty letter, the Boss might decide that's the last order for your company!

So in all letters dealing with discounts taken incorrectly, use good judgment, tact, and sometimes humor.

You might write:

There are several ways, Mrs. Cooke . .

of saying thank you to our good customers . . . with our product, through our service—and by giving a discount when bills are paid within 10 days.

And, frankly, when customers pay promptly, it helps us to make similar savings in our purchases. On the other hand, if they don't, we lose the benefit of such savings—and then we just can't allow any discount.

Because you've been such a good customer we'd like to allow the $45 discount on your last purchase. But that wouldn't be fair to others who did pay within 10 days. So, we're sorry, and hope you understand.

Don't bother to send us a check now; we'll just add the discounted amount to your next invoice. It will save you some paperwork.

Many thanks . . .

Another technique is to "make light" of the situation.

Tempest really fugits, Mrs. Sileno . .

and that's probably why you didn't realize the bill for the typewriters was paid too late to take advantage of our 10-day discount privilege.

I'm sorry. But don't be concerned. Rather than troubling you to send us a check, we'll just add the $10 difference to your next bill.

Of course, if you prefer handling it another way, just let me know.

Sincerely,

More and more companies are giving discounts . . . even some department stores on personal charge accounts. So if your volume of Discount Letters is increasing, don't be alarmed . . . play it cool, rely on your customer's sense of fair play . . . and develop several good letters for all circumstances.

8.

I'm writing to inquire...

There isn't much of a trick to writing a letter of inquiry. You simply decide what you want to know, write it down . . . as concisely and clearly as possible.

Unless you get straight to the point—don't be vague, please— several things could happen:

▶your letter won't be read

▶the reader might have to write back and ask you what you meant; this is sometimes embarrassing, sometimes insulting

▶the answer might give far more detail than you wanted, because the respondent is guessing what you want.

None of these results is good. They waste time and cause delays. So make things simple . . .

► state in the opening sentence the subject of your inquiry

► for each item of information you want, use a separate paragraph

► unless you're asking for confidential information, and need to justify your request, don't overplay why you want the information. Few people care.

Here's an example how *not* to do it:

Dear Sirs:

Just the other day my neighbor, Mrs. Myrtle, mentioned how nice a table would look on my patio. Not just any table, she said, but a nice wooden one. Of course, wood would be necessary to go with the siding of the house and all the trees in the yard.

My husband planted those trees years ago . . about twenty, I guess. It's so sad he didn't live to see them grow.

My patio isn't terribly big, so the table shouldn't be large . . just a medium-size one would do nicely.

And of course I wouldn't want to spend too much on it. Herman's pension and insurance left me nicely taken care of, but one mustn't be extravagant.

Do you have something nice that you think I might like? I hope so. Mrs. Myrtle and I would like to have the table soon so we can have coffee outside during the warm weather.

Sincerely,

The sales manager will have a great time with that letter asking for a medium-size wooden table that doesn't cost too much. It would be interesting to know what he did, but he won't tell.

Here are some better letters:

Dear Mr. Manger:

Would you be willing to share your experience as founder and editor of a quarterly magazine?

Specifically, I'd like to know:

what objectives the magazine is designed to meet,

the editorial policy which has been set, and

your method of evaluating the success of your magazine.

Any information you can give us will be a tremendous help in planning a magazine we hope to launch here.

Many thanks for your time and help.

Appreciatively,

Dear Mr. Gordon:

I'd appreciate your help in preparing an article about marketing by major corporations.

The article will deal with shifts in advertising strategy over the past five years . . shifts to meet changes in consumer attitudes, preferences and buying power.

If the information is available for publication, I'd be interested in knowing how your advertising strategy . . the copy platform, media mix and frequency . . has changed over the past five years, and the reasons for the changes.

Since the article will be illustrated, it would also be helpful if you could send reproduction proofs of different ads that illustrate both your current campaign and that run five years ago.

We'll certainly appreciate any information you can give us.

Many thanks,

One important point to remember in writing letters of inquiry is to avoid being negative . . . it's okay to be polite, but don't be totally humble. That is, don't say things like:

I know I shouldn't take your valuable time

I don't want to inconvenience you

I realize I'm imposing, but . . .

Phrases like that are a red flag . . . they offer an excuse for the reader not to do what you want him to do.

"I'M WRITING TO REPLY . . ."

Now that you've seen how to write a letter of inquiry, you'll want to know how to answer one . . . especially one that is like the vague inquiry about wooden tables.

Letters of inquiry come from three basic sources:

►people who are seriously interested in your product or services;

►those who are interested but are shopping around;

►those who are sort of interested but mostly just curious.

When you don't know what prompts the inquiry, you must assume the person is interested but shopping. Therefore, your answer should go out before the competition's, and it should sell.

Here are some rules:

►*Be prompt.* If someone is interested enough to write for information, he can be sold. Make sure you get your answer out quickly. Anyway, even if you don't want to sell anything, it's rude to keep people waiting for answers.

▶*Be specific.* Answer the questions . . . if you can figure out what they are . . . and give enough detail to convince the person that your product or service is the best available. If you want to include more detail than you can comfortably handle in a letter, enclose a catalogue or specification sheet and refer to it.

▶*Be polite.* True, many inquiries are not well-thought-out (to put it mildly). But the person who made the inquiry didn't know he was vague, and you shouldn't expect him to know . . . if he knew as much about your business as you do, he'd be in it. So, assume the question(s) are in good faith and be patient.

▶*Say "thank you."* Inquiries represent a great source of business. Obviously, not every inquirer will buy something, but how do you tell in advance? You can't lose if you assume everyone will buy, and treat them as if the sale was about to be made. Isn't it natural to say thank you to someone who has bought something from you?

Here's how *not* to answer a letter of inquiry:

Dear Mr. Davis:

I assume that what you really want to know is the cost of our consulting services when you are seeking a new job. I say assume because, frankly, your letter was vague and I can't be sure.

The attached sheets explain our service in detail. I suggest you read them and if you are then still interested, call my secretary and she will try to make an appointment for you.

I would like to point out that our fee is payable when we are contracted, and not when you find a new job.

Sincerely,

That letter was written by a guy who's had it all his own way for too long. Otherwise, he'd have written it this way:

Dear Mr. Davis:

We'd be delighted to talk with you and work out a strategy for finding you a new job.

At this point it's hard to say what the cost would be, because the fee is based on a combination of what you presently earn and the type of position you hope to attain.

I've tentatively put you down for an appointment on Thursday of next week at noon. I realize how hard it is to search and be discreet, so lunch hour is usually the best time to chat. If that isn't convenient for you, please call me and we'll set another time.

Thanks very much for contacting me. I'll look forward to meeting and talking with you next Thursday.

                                        Cordially,

Here's another good reply:

Dear Mr. Dalton:

We do, indeed, have a punctureproof tire. They're available in a size to fit your Ford wagon and the price is only $25 per tire.

I've enclosed a brochure which describes how these tires are made, and the mileage and safety advantages for you and your family. Also enclosed are the names of dealers in your area.

We believe that these tires are the best available anywhere. When you've driven on them we know you'll agree.

Thanks for writing.

                                        Happy Motoring!

There may be times when you have to refuse information . . . for competitive reasons, etc. When that happens, be honest. Don't make excuses. Just say the information isn't available, and tell why. For example:

Dear Mr. Frost:

I'm terribly sorry we won't be able to give you the marketing information for your article.

As you know, this is a highly competitive industry. If the information you requested became public, it would prove very valuable to our competitors and seriously hamper our sales efforts.

We do appreciate your desire to include us in your article. If you need other information—of a less sensitive nature—we'll be glad to provide it. I'll await word from you. Good luck with your project.

Cordially,

Dear Mr. Harrelson:

I regret to say it, but the information you requested isn't available.

Our safety department records the number and cost of accidents, but we don't know the man-hours lost and their cost in lost productivity.

Sorry I can't be of more help.

Cordially,

In Bear Creek Orchards, Oregon, Harry and David are owners of The Fruit-of-the-Month Club. They answer inquiries in such interesting ways, it makes you want to ask a question just to get their answer!

Recently a customer's monthly fruit package had been broken into before delivery. The fruit that had not been taken was spoiled. She wrote asking what could be done about it.

Harry and David wrote:

It's sort of a left-handed compliment,

Mrs. Smith,

that by the time your gift package reached you it had proved just too tempting to someone along the way.

We're sorry and embarrassed, of course.

Since the shipping season for peaches has ended, we'll send Crisp Mountain Apples at Thanksgiving in replacement.

We hope this will make up for the disappointment expressed in your letter.

Best wishes,

There isn't any trick to writing or answering letters of inquiry—

Determine what you want to know, or tell

then

Write it down.

9.

I have a complaint...

There's nothing more likely to ruin a potentially beautiful day than a complaint . . . some guy with a chip on his shoulder, itching to make you miserable. He doesn't stop to consider that his complaint may be unjustified—90% of the time, anyway—and poof, there goes your good mood.

Of course, too many of us in business don't stop to consider that the fella seldom knows his complaint is unjustified. Most complaints are sincere expressions of displeasure.

And when you answer a complaint, the object is not to tell someone he's a fool . . . the object is to get him back on your team—appease him—woo him. Explain the situation; point out the misunderstanding; let him know just how far your company will go to clear things up.

Of course, if the complaint is justified—if your outfit is in the wrong—admit it and don't try to make excuses. Excuses don't win friends; honesty and interest in the other person's feelings do. And business can always use friendly customers.

As a matter of fact, complaints are often blessings in disguise. They can pinpoint trouble areas and give us an early chance to zoom in and lick the problem before it grows.

Public relations departments of many companies thrive on letters, calls or visits from customers with a complaint. Clifford B. Reeves, one of the leading public relations men in the financial field, describes public relations as:

> finding out what people like about you and doing more of it; and finding out what they don't like and doing less of it.

Customer complaints give us these opportunities.

Here are some guidelines for dealing with such letters:

▶*Answer them right away.* Complaints are one of the nerves connecting you to your customer. Don't let a little ache become a big pain by neglecting it. Let the customer know you're investigating his story, even if only by a brief card.

▶*Investigate thoroughly.* Get your facts and *get them all* before you make any judgments. Snap decisions can be wrong, and wrong decisions place you in the uncomfortable position of having to reverse yourself.

▶*If you're wrong—admit it.* Never forget that a part of the American psyche is geared to rally to the underdog. The surest way to get the customer back on your side is to be frank . . . admit an error.

▶*Never argue.* Arguments tend to degenerate into name calling . . . and all that does is embarrass someone. Even if you win the argument, you lose . . . you lose a customer.

▶*Tell the customer enough to satisfy him.* If you can't fill his request completely, he has a right to know why. And if his complaint is unfounded, he has a right to know why. Don't hide behind rules or operating policies; use straightforward language and enough detail to make your position clear.

▶*Be courteous.* (Even if it means biting your tongue.) The customer is interested in himself and his problem. And he'll be more easily appeased if he thinks you're interested in him and his problem. A courteous tone will go a long way to solving any differences.

Now that the wisdom of the rules has been set down, let's look at examples of complaints and answers.

"I simply asked . . ."

Most people who make a claim, honestly think they've got it coming, and feel they have a right to question a decision which went against them. While you may be familiar with all the rules of your business, your customers aren't—even if they should be.

Take the young wife who banged up her car coming from a bridge game. You can imagine what her husband had to say! But they did have insurance, and they figured it would all be taken care of.

And then the insurance appraisal came—$100 less than the amount the garage wanted to fix the car! Young wife sat right down and wrote her agent:

Dear Mr. Risk:

There must be some mistake. Today I received your insurance appraisal for the damage to my car and you show that you will pay only $175 of the $275 the garage is charging!

We have been paying premiums to your company for the past five years, and never had a claim. So we think you should pay for the entire bill.

My husband is angry enough over this little accident, but if he doesn't get the correct amount of insurance for the damage, I hate to think how angry he'll be.

Please take another look at the costs for repairs to the car, and send me a revised figure of the amount you will pay. I hope to hear from you quickly.

Sincerely,

Louise Driver

Now true, this is a complaint . . . but the kind we classify as "I simply asked . . ." Nothing bitter—no name calling—just an honest question.

And Mrs. Driver really believes there is an error in her appraisal—an honest mistake. She simply forgot, or doesn't understand, about the $100 deductible clause in her policy. (For those who are not familiar with this clause, it simply means that the car owner pays any costs incurred up to the amount of the deductible—in this case $100. The insurance company pays that part of the costs over the $100 deductible.)

So, because by this Chapter you're a great letter writer, you recognize Mrs. Driver's predicament and write:

I know exactly how you feel, Mrs. Driver . . .

the same thing happened to me some years ago. And you know what the problem was? I'd forgotten we had a $100 deductible clause in our policy.

At the time you purchased your policy, you surely didn't expect any accidents. And by including the $100 deductible, you saved quite a few dollars in premiums each year. In fact, over the years you have had this coverage you have already saved in premiums much more than the $100! Your decision to take the deductible was a good one.

I wish I had better news for you, but I'm sure your husband will understand just as soon as you explain. After all, he forgot, too.

I hope your car looks as good as new, and that from now on you'll have nothing but—

Happy Driving.

Remember, don't fault people for lack of knowledge. Nobody knows everything. In fact, all things considered, very few among us know very much at all. Including me—and thee.

Instant gripes

Remember some other things about complaints. Many of them result from impulse . . . we call them "instant gripes."

The customer thinks he's been stepped on . . . he flushes and releases his ire in a hasty, mean, nasty letter:

> Gentlemen?
>
> You really blew the deal. What do you mean billing me for three outstanding invoices, when I paid one of them two weeks ago? Did you think I'd pay all three again?
>
> You big companies are all alike. Think you can put something over on us little guys. Well now you can wait for the money on the other two.
>
> I. M. Maad

It's off his chest, and he feels better. But the next day he might not even remember what he wrote—and if he does, he's surely cooled off a great deal. That's what we mean—the gripe lasts only an instant. You'd better not anger him all over again with an offensive reply. (The customer can afford to be hasty—your business can't.)

So relax . . . buzz for your secretary . . . and in your calmest manner dictate:

> And you have every right, Mr. Maad . . .
>
> to be concerned about the invoices. Most certainly we were wrong in sending three when you'd already paid one.
>
> Please accept our regrets. We'll do all we can to see it doesn't happen again.
>
> Apologetically,
>
> P.S. And when you feel we've served our penance and waited long enough, we'd appreciate your check for just $78.91— the total of the two remaining bills.

A reply such as this is much more effective than if you'd tried to out-nasty Mr. Maad.

Hotels often receive complaints from guests.

> Manager:
>
> The room I stayed in last night in your hotel was a mess. It hadn't been properly cleaned in weeks. You'd better never put me up in Room 517 again. That is, if I ever stay at your hotel again.
>
> > M. E. Klean

Of course, the room wasn't half as bad as he said—but it's human nature to exaggerate when we're annoyed. Now the manager might be inclined to tell this customer where he can go next time—but that just isn't good business. So very wisely he writes:

> I have to agree with you, Mr. Klean . . .
>
> the room you occupied with us was not up to our standards. I had the housekeeper inspect it with me and you can be sure there'll be no problem staying in Room 517 again.
>
> Thank you so much for bringing this to our attention. And please forgive us for making your stay less pleasant than it should have been. I hope you will give us another chance.
>
> > Apologetically,

A letter like this should bring Mr. Klean back to the hotel— because the situation was so well handled—and also to check up on room 517! (But make sure you've really corrected the situation.)

In the life insurance business, where one individual often holds several policies, mass mailings to policyholders can present the problem of how to send only one copy of a message to each insured. Companies spend much time and money to eliminate duplicates, because policyholders are sensitive to the wasted expense of postage and printing.

At Mutual Of New York, weeding out duplicates of the Annual Report used to be manual . . . but now, like most things, it's a computer operation and the problem of more than one Report to a policyholder has, in large part, been overcome. However, some do slip through and—

when MONY gets a message such as:

Mr. President:

For your information, I received three reports in the mail. I should think one would be enough. Stop wasting the policyholders' money.

Miss Policyholder

MONY answers:

You are absolutely right, Miss Policyholder . . .

and we do try to eliminate the duplicates for policyholders with more than one policy. Unfortunately our machines slipped up this time.

You see, one of the big steps that electronics has helped us make is to weed out as many duplicates as possible, when we mail our Annual Report. And to be perfectly honest, it's done a pretty good job—but it isn't yet foolproof.

I'm sorry . . . but I do appreciate your taking the time to let us know we haven't quite buttoned up all the possible errors.

Thanks so much,

And here's a priceless exchange of complaint correspondence between a disgruntled commuter and his railroad—

Gentlemen:

I have been riding trains daily for the past two years and the service over your lines seems to be getting worse every day.

I am getting tired of standing in the aisle all the time on a 50 mile trip. I think the transportation is worse than that enjoyed by the people two thousand years ago.

Dear Sir:

We received your letter with reference to the shortcomings of our service and believe you are somewhat confused in your history. The only mode of transportation two thousand years ago was by foot.

Gentlemen:

I am in receipt of your letter and I think you are the one who is confused in your history.

If you will refer to the Bible, Book of David, 9th Chapter, you will find that Aaron rode into town on his ass. THAT, gentlemen, is something I have not been able to do on your trains for the past two years.

"Something's wrong . . ."

Very like the complaint letter, is the letter which asks for some kind of adjustment—wrong product; incorrect size; article missing.

It's astonishing how many people are aware we live in an imperfect world, yet are unwilling to admit that they can make mistakes. So when a letter comes in from a customer saying their company goofed—that some adjustment is due —they see red and cuss the customer who is so unreasonable.

Now maybe they've got a point . . . sometimes customers are unreasonable. But that doesn't matter. If the customer *thinks* he's due an adjustment, you've the job of writing a letter that keeps him happy . . . even if he's wrong.

The guidelines are the same as for complaints—

►Investigate thoroughly

►Answer right away

►Admit it—if you're wrong

►Never argue

►Be courteous

Here are a few examples that apply to all these guides . . .

Dear Mr. Eiler:

I have your Complaint Department form asking about the most recent of my missing sheets. This time a contour sheet. (However, in its place was another contour sheet and inside was stamped the name of the owner. Naturally, I returned this to your driver.)

In July, when my last sheet was lost, you suggested I count my articles before the laundry left each week—and your people would count it, too, before it left your shop. You can see that isn't working—seems the count is right, but the sheets are wrong!

As I told you before, my sheets are custom-made by the W. Bedding Company. Replacing them is expensive and aggravating. And at the rate your laundry is losing them, very shortly I won't have any left.

This is absolutely your last chance. I expect your check to replace the sheet. Unless, of course, I'm fortunate enough to have it returned. And the next time anything is missing from my laundry, I'll have to change company.

Sorry,

Mrs. R. A. Blanket

Dear Mrs. Blanket:

I'm afraid your excellent taste in linens may be our undoing. Someone obviously thinks they go well in her home, because the missing sheets were never returned.

Saying "we're sorry" doesn't help, I know. You are still minus the sheets. But I hope the action I've taken will show you our real concern. Rather than put you to the trouble, I phoned the W. Bedding Company, explained the situation, and asked them to immediately make a set of your sheets and send them to you—with our apologies. They promise to get them out within the next 2 weeks . . . of course, at our expense.

If I could make a positive statement that "it won't happen again," I'd be the happiest guy in the laundry business. But all I can do is tell you we'll try not to let it—and hope you understand.

Thanks for your patience,

O. V. Eiler

Gentlemen:

Three weeks ago I ordered from your gourmet shop a case of 4 oz. jars of olives stuffed with anchovies. I had previously tasted them at a friend's home and found them delicious.

Now I have opened 3 bottles—and none taste as good as those my friend served. There must be something wrong with this particular case, because it is the same brand.

So I want to have a driver pick up the balance of the case and return it to you. And because they did not taste good, I will expect the cost of the full case credited to my account.

Sincerely,

Earl Tasty

We're sorry you were disappointed, Mr. Tasty . . .

and really quite surprised. This particular brand is our biggest seller. In fact, yours is the very first complaint we have had.

But, of course, if you're not satisfied we would not want you to keep the balance of the case. Our driver will pick them up on Monday at 10:30 A.M.

Your account will be credited for the nine bottles returned. I'm sure you can appreciate that although the 3 bottles of olives did not meet your expectations, as long as they were used we cannot credit you for those.

May I make a suggestion? The next time you order an "unusual item" order only a small quantity . . then, if it pleases you we can send the balance at the "case price." We'd certainly be happy to do that for you.

Again, my apologies.

Gourmet Manager
Cacy Department Store

Looking at things from the customer's point of view, there are some adjustment requests that are just as clever as can be.

Here's one—written after considerable mixup with a subscription to *Playboy* magazine:

Gentlemen:

Why don't bunnies like me?

I've paid my subscription; renewed each year for the past three; praised all the issues I've read . . but all of a sudden, I'm neglected.

When I came back to college in September, I notified you of my change of address so the magazine would reach me here. It usually arrived the 20th of the month . . so get this picture—

October 20—10 fraternity brothers waiting patiently for the mailman. He comes in sight—all 10 start for him like a locust rush. He dodges and darts, then throws in the bag (mailbag, that is). All 10 brothers pounce on it—but no *Playboy*.

November 20—Same scene. Same result.

December 20—No one believes I have a subscription!

Won't you help me before January 20?

Take a look at your subscription records or address changes or something—but find out what's happening to my magazine.

And get hoppin', Bunny, please. Our mailman is getting ragged!

Frustrated,

Easy to write this way? Easy to speak softly—yet wish you could swing a big stick?

Yes—it is if you'll keep in mind two important things:

Handle people as you want to be handled in a similar situation

and

Remember, an unhappy customer may ruin your day . . . but enough unhappy customers can ruin your business.

10.

Follow-up letters to end follow-up

Obviously, letters have a purpose. A letter is a failure if it doesn't achieve its intention.

Maybe the letter lacked interest value, or was difficult to read; maybe it didn't generate a sense of urgency in the reader; perhaps it was vague. Whatever the reason, letters that don't work need to be followed up.

Before writing a follow-up, try to determine what went wrong with your first effort . . . otherwise, you might not do any better the second time. Or the third time.

This, of course, means you must recognize that your letter could have been at fault—not the person who didn't answer. Once you've determined why the letter failed, here are some traps to avoid in the follow-up.

Use some tact. Don't point fingers and blame the reader for not having answered.

Why haven't you had the courtesy to answer my earlier letter?

Waiting for your answer to our letter is trying our patience.

We still haven't heard from you.

These statements are forbidden. Blaming the other guy, even if he is to blame, will put him on the defensive—and that won't make him want to cooperate in giving you the result you want.

Never, never repeat the first letter. If it didn't click at first, there's no reason to think it'll work any better the second time.

Structure follow-up letters differently. The opening, for example, should have an extraordinary amount of emphasis . . . to create interest quickly. Make it short—and to the point.

Follow-up letters must be different—or they could end up in the "round file"—like the original.

Here's a collection of follow-ups on varied subjects . . . but they're letters which got the action the writer was looking for. They're unusual . . . attention-getting . . . action-provoking!

Upside Down! . . . from a company to a salesman

OK, Bob. I'm standing on my head* and I don't practice Yoga.

Now will you get the signed receipt—please?

*figuratively—of course!

To a slow-moving repairman

Patience was never one of my virtues, Mr. Coe . . .

but all of a sudden I'm beginning to feel very virtuous. It's been 3 weeks now since you promised to deliver the parts to repair my air conditioner, and although I haven't heard from you, I've still remained a patient man.

But this note is to let you know that patience is wearing thin . . especially after this past week when the temperatures floated between 85° and 90°.

Now you wouldn't want to spoil my record, would you? If you can have the parts here no later than Wednesday morning, I can keep calm. A phone call from you tomorrow, to confirm that you'll be here, will keep me waiting . .

Patiently,

To a tardy furniture dealer

You're batting .500, Mr. Glickman . . .

and I suppose that isn't bad this early in the season. One-half of my order for the new desk chairs has arrived.

But no word came with them about when the second half could be expected. (As a matter of fact, I expected them all to arrive together.) Has something happened?

Please let me know by next Friday when the rest will be here. You can imagine the morale problem it will cause if half the employees get new chairs and half don't.

Hurry,

To an indifferent doctor

You've left your patient uncovered, Doctor . . .

because without your assurance he is in good health, we can't issue the health insurance policy he requested.

Attached is a duplicate of the form we sent you on April 10 (in case yours has been misplaced). Won't you take a few minutes to fill it in, and ask your secretary to mail it today.

Unfortunately, there's a deadline, Doctor. If Mr. Hill's medical history doesn't reach us by next Wednesday, May 16, he will have to reapply for his insurance. So . . .

Thanks for your help,

And another one

Your patient has only 9 days left, Doctor . . .

9 days in which to get his life insurance at its present rate. After that, Mr. Well will be in the next "insurance age bracket" and his premium will go up.

Won't you please fill out the medical form we sent you 3 weeks ago, and mail it to me immediately. (In case it's been misplaced, here is another copy.)

Your patient will be very grateful.

Many thanks,

And a third

Would you help the doctor, Miss Nurse . . .

by taking some of the work off his shoulders? And at the same time, you'd be helping me.

Two weeks ago, I asked the doctor to fill out two medical forms for my insurance company, and I haven't received them. Frankly, I am quite anxious to get the refund due me.

I know how very busy the doctor is, but perhaps you can shuffle some of the papers on his desk, find mine, and ask him to fill it in.

Will you, please?

Appreciatively,

From a fund-raiser

Remember 1968, Mr. Riloff?

the year of unbelievable, unnecessary tragedy in our country. How many times during that year did you ask—

How can I, as an individual, help?

What little share of the responsibility for my fellow men can I assume?

Where do I begin?

Three weeks ago, I wrote asking for your contribution to the Hospital Fund. I haven't yet heard from you, perhaps because you just haven't had the time.

But here's where you can begin, Mr. Riloff—your check for any amount at all will be an excellent start. Will you send it, soon?

Thanks so much,

To a busy college placement officer

Dear Mr. White:

Transcripts, transcripts . . you must be flooded with requests for them. My letter of August 1 asked for one, too, on Steve Brion, class of 1969.

Normally, I would wait my turn, but am in a bind on this one. Pressure is coming from two sides—the department that wants to hire Steve immediately, and from Steve himself. The problem is we can't make a job offer without a copy of his transcript.

Could you pull our request from the pile and give it your special attention? It's needed by the 14th if we are going to offer him the job.

I'll be most appreciative if you can meet this deadline. And I feel sure Steve will be too.

Many thanks,

For an overdue premium

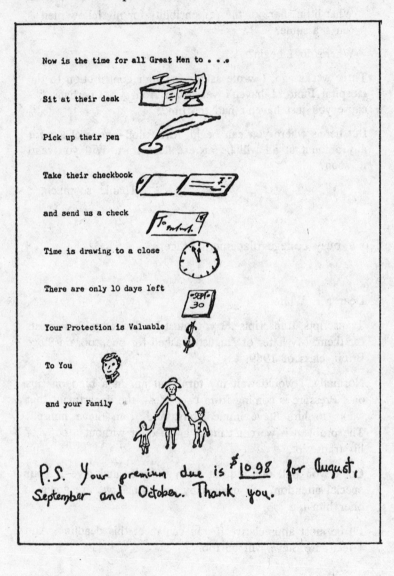

Now is the time for all Great Men to . . .

Sit at their desk

Pick up their pen

Take their checkbook

and send us a check

Time is drawing to a close

There are only 10 days left

Your Protection is Valuable

To You

and your Family

P.S. Your premium due is $10.98 for August, September and October. Thank you.

From a business machines manufacturer

How is your calculator working, Mr. Jackson?

By the way, ours is working very well, and after adding up all your payments, we find there is only one payment outstanding on your calculating machine.

It's the one for $12.26 which I wrote you about last month, remember?

Why not put your check in the mail today, so I'll have it by September 12—and the calculator will be all yours.

Thank you,

To a "Mating" Machine that didn't!

To: OPERATION "MATCH"

Am I, Dear Computer . . .

Unmatchable?

Heaven Forbid! But, it's been over a month since I sent you my cherished application and not a word have I received.

So what can I think, dear machine—except that there is no other sweet little blue card (for BOY) which joins my own little pink card (for GIRL) in harmonious bliss.

I'll accept my fate—the life of a single—in the modern day of Match, Catch, Click and all the technical join-togethers. But, before you cast me to my desolate destiny, holy machine . . .

Send back my four dollars!

The Case of the Perk-less Percolator

Gentlemen:

Did you ever try making coffee in a coffeepot that consisted of only the pot and top . . no insides or glass top!!

Well, I'm afraid I just might have to try unless you send me the parts I requested a few weeks ago. Remember? I had received the 8-cup coffeepot April 6—but all that arrived was the pot and top—no stem, basket, basket top or glass top!

If you don't send the missing parts quickly, my family could grow to like instant coffee. Then where would that leave you? . . .

. . . Huh?

The insurance industry probably writes more letters than almost any other industry. And letters for overdue premiums lead the list. Here's one that pulls out all the stops:

Dear Mr. O'Grady:

Does your wife know about GRACE?

If she did, she'd probably be after you, like we are, to pay your August life insurance premium. Twenty days of your GRACE period have already gone by. Both she and you have a lot at stake in this policy and I'm sure neither of you would like to see it lapse. (And frankly, that's the last thing we want to happen, too.)

So what can you lose? Okay, let's tally up some of the things at stake if you ignore our friendly nudging and let the policy lapse:

1. Your loved ones—the beneficiaries—will be deprived of a $10,000 nest egg you set aside with the stroke of your pen, just 5 years ago.

2. Your hard-earned cash investment of $867 in premiums will be lost. (Well not exactly, because we could pay you the $550 cash value or convert it into a paid-up $1,300 insurance policy.)

3. You will have to provide medical evidence of insurability if you should ever decide to purchase insurance again.

4. Your rates for new insurance would naturally be considerably higher; the older you get, the higher the premium.

Now honestly, you wouldn't want to lose all those advantages, would you?

Frankly, this is a follow-up, and we are just assuming that you *did* receive the first notice that your premium was due by August 1. If this is not the case, please tell us right away. Or if something unexpected is making it difficult for you to pay at this time, let us know; we might be able to work out some arrangement to prevent your losing this protection.

Time is running out, and we'll need to hear from you before the lapse date of September 1. How about doing yourself and your family a favor . . . it'll only take a minute.

Sincerely,

P.S. I'll let you explain GRACE to your wife.

Got the picture? Do you see the value of follow-up openings that are . . .

> *different*
>
> *disarming*
>
> *unanticipated* . . .

11.

Potpourri

As the title suggests, this is a catchall chapter. It is presented as an alternative to an almost endless list of categories of letters.

Yet, most letters in this chapter have something in common . . . they're designed to build good will for the person and company sending them. That's because they're "volunteer letters"—letters that didn't *have* to be written. And one of the best ways to build good will is to do something pleasant when it's not expected.

What occasions will these letters fit? Many—anniversaries, new babies, compliments to employees, holiday greetings, birthdays, promotions, personal touches from top management, retirements, sales records, welcome to new employees.

In addition, there are two other categories of letters in this chapter: recruiting sales help and fund raising. They're here to—

(1) justify the name of the chapter,

(2) because we couldn't figure where else to put them.

Please understand, writing these letters is not an insidious attempt to increase your work load. It's merely an example of how you can put a smile on a face and a good thought in a head.

Good thoughts come in handy. Like money in the bank.

Anniversaries

CONGRATULATIONS ON EMPLOYEE ANNIVERSARY

Dear Jim:

It only seems like yesterday when you joined us, but the calendar tells the tale. My best wishes on your twentieth year with our company.

During these years you've seen the expansion that has taken place—and surely, you've gotten much personal satisfaction in being part of that development.

My very best to you on this big day.

Congratulations,

CONGRATULATIONS TO CUSTOMER
ON ANNIVERSARY OF
DOING BUSINESS TOGETHER

You know, Jim . . .

last week was a milestone in our association: ten years of doing business together.

Often we overlook the loyalty and friendships in business which mean so much to us. But I wanted to be sure to take this occasion to say a heartfelt "thank you" for the confidence you've expressed in me over the years.

I hope we'll see many more years together,

Sincerely,

A new baby, or, bundles from heaven

FIRST BABY

Dear Floss and Mel:

Glad to hear you've joined the 2:00 A.M. club! And don't let anyone tell you differently—it's worth it.

The hours are long . . but the job as parent just can't be beaten. It's the greatest, most rewarding in the world.

As soon as you've had a chance to get acquainted with your new daughter, we'll be over to visit.

Fondly,

Great News, Glen . .

a son and heir! A crown prince! I can just imagine how pleased you and Betsy are.

When do I get my cigar? Come to think of it, I should buy you a drink—and I will the next time we get together.

A hug to your wife and son.

Best,

SECOND, THIRD OR FIFTH

You've a full house, Marge and Bob . .

and a mighty nice one. And I'll bet the whole family is acting as though the new baby is the first.

The nice part of "other than first children" is that you're no longer scared . . you know they can't break—and they eat and sleep when they want. So you really can enjoy them. Get to it. And we'll be over soon to get a look at his highness.

Congratulations,

TENTH??

What can we say, Bill and Bette . . .

that we haven't said in our last nine notes? Maybe just . . .
good luck!

With love,

Compliments to employees of other companies

TO THE BOSS ABOUT HIS RECEPTIONIST

Dear Mr. Koke:

A lovely smile . . a cheerful "good morning" . . and a "may
I take your coat?" made yesterday one of those days when
all was right with the world.

And, Mr. Koke, your receptionist did the trick! Please thank
her for me.

Appreciatively,

TO THE BOSS ABOUT HIS SECRETARY

You're a lucky man, Mr. O'Connor . . .

Miss Martel is a prime candidate for an award on how a
secretary can "win friends and influence people!"

Her enthusiasm and complete delight are contagious . . and
frankly carried with me throughout the day.

I couldn't resist dropping you this note. She is a treasure.

Enviously,

Holiday greetings

Dear Mr. Wales:

The end of the year will be here soon, and I wanted you to know what a pleasure it was serving you during the past months. Customers such as you have made it possible for us to grow steadily and rapidly. I hope our service has been able to contribute, in turn, to the growth and success of your business.

Thanks again for your confidence in us. I hope you and your family have a wonderful holiday season and a prosperous new year.

Appreciatively,

It's a peaceful time of year, David . . .

a time to sit back and think about all the good things to be thankful for . . . like friends and associates such as you.

The business you've given us in the past year is more than appreciated; it's been fun working with you.

I hope you and your family have a wonderful time together over the holidays. To all of you we send the hope that the coming year will be rewarding.

All the best,

Birthday

Greetings . . .

and Happy Birthday. I'd like to join your many other friends, in telling you what a genuine pleasure it is to know and do business with you.

And with greetings comes the wish that you may enjoy many more years of health, happiness and success.

Sincerely,

Birthdays come in all sizes—and numbers!

And they come to all people—but some wear them far better than others. Happy Birthday, you're in the lead!

Although we've known each other a good number of years, to me you are just the same as when I first met you. That takes a very special talent. Don't ever lose it.

Here's to your 100th!

Promotions or transfers

TO A PERSONAL FRIEND

Congrats, Jamie . . .

on the latest move up. You go any higher in that organization and I'll have to make an appointment to say good morning.

Seriously, I know how hard you've worked for this, and it's good to see it come through.

I'm really pleased.

Keep it up!

TO THE WIFE OF A PERSONAL FRIEND

Dear Beth:

It's been said, "Behind every successful man stands a woman." So, I'm giving applause where it's really due . . to you.

Congratulations, Beth! Helping Gene reach Vice President is a tremendous compliment to you. But with your talent and ability behind him, I'm not surprised.

Best of Luck,

TO A PERSONAL FRIEND—AND HIS WIFE

Dear Don:

Please give Jane my best and also my congratulations. While you've done a great job and deserve your new title . . let's face it . . it's really the woman behind the man.

Best to both of you . .

P.S. Honestly, Don, I'm delighted for you.

TO A MALE—FROM A FEMALE

Dear Bud:

Before the meeting where we first were introduced, Bob told me you were a guy to keep an eye on. (Frankly, being female, I found it very easy to do!)

But after reading about your promotion, I see his meaning was different than mine. Still, my sincerest wishes.

Congratulations!

P.S. Mind if I still keep an eye on you . . and your future with the company?

PROMOTED—MOVING TO ANOTHER CITY

Dear Gil:

Chicago's gain is sure New York's loss. But, since it means such a nice opportunity, we'll have to pout and bear it.

Seriously, you have all my good wishes for a great job in your new position.

Keep in touch—

Dear Vaughan:

Don't let "out of sight—out of mind" apply to us. Even though lady fortune smilingly sent you to Los Angeles for your new job, keep in touch.

You deserve this break . . you've done an exceptional job here. You're headed right for the top. And I for one am rooting you on.

Congratulations!

TO SOMEONE WHO'S HAD SEVERAL PROMOTIONS

You've done it again, Dick . . .

and this time it's a top prize—Vice President. Guess I'll start now to write my note for when you get the Presidency!

I might have said this before but, as always, the best of luck and success in your new venture.

Congratulations!

TO CONGRATULATE MANAGEMENT ON ITS SELECTION

Probably, Joe . . .

one of the reasons your organization is tops in its field is because it employs only the best. And you've done it again . . Kelly Anderson.

My congratulations on being able to spirit him away from his old firm—and you've really got a star on your hands. I've known and worked with Kelly for many years and have never known anyone who didn't think he was great.

I know you'll enjoy having him aboard.

Sincerely,

TO THE BOSS WHEN HE'S MOVING ON UP

Dear Mr. Rees:

A week ago today, when your new appointment was announced, there was such an air of mixed emotions it was almost impossible to sort them.

All of us are so happy to see the recognition given you— but all of us are quite selfish about losing "our boss." Now, a week later, the emotions are the same . . we can't really believe you will ever be gone from us.

In the years I have been with you, there's been much evidence of the wisdom and kindness that, along with your unusual abilities, make you a rare and wonderful person with whom to be associated. It was a privilege to work with you.

I hope you will be happy in your new office—I know you will be successful in accomplishing your objectives.

Most sincerely,

THANK-YOU NOTE FOR CONGRATULATIONS

Dear Mark:

If I am seen sneaking out of the building within the next day or two, my mission will be to purchase a picture frame.

What for? To put your heart-warming letter in. Your kind remarks are most generous . . and I genuinely appreciate them.

Thank you,

With friends such as you, Jim . .

wishing me well, how can I miss? You've put me on the proverbial spot—and I'll just have to make good.

Thanks so much for all your wishes.

Most sincerely,

NICE TOUCHES FROM TOP MANAGEMENT

A year-end report . . . mailed to the employee at his home, from the president of the corporation.

Dear Bob:

I don't want to let the arrival of the new year pass without wishing you and your family my hope that all of us may enjoy a peaceful and productive new year.

At this time last year, we were able to look back upon twelve months of almost uninterrupted and extremely profitable progress. It wasn't easy to maintain that pace. It was for us, as for many American corporations, a mixed year. We've had to work very hard, but the good has outweighed the bad.

(Here followed a financial report of the year)

Our business demands much of every individual who is part of it. If you set your goals and work to your planned objectives, no set of problems should prevent us from setting new records.

Happy New Year to you and yours.

Sincerely,

An unusual letter from the Home Office (located in New York City) to its branch offices all over the country . . . during the New York transit strike.

Our service operations have been "Quilled" . . .

and as of immediately, we need your mostest and bestest cooperation, patience and indulgence.

The entire transportation system of New York City has been most effectively tied up by a strike. The net result is that despite numerous innovations by management, we are getting only 70/75% of our people to work. And you don't have to be an actuary to figure that 70/75% of the people can't do 100% of the work—especially with the added load of year-end closing . . a major operation in itself.

You can be assured that everyone who can get to the Home Office is working to maintain the company's high standard of service. Keep in mind, too, that we'll stay on the job—since once in New York it's equally difficult to get home!

Seriously, tho, the situation is quite rough. And while every possible effort is being made—it's almost inevitable that there will be some service delays. We merely ask that you try to understand . . that you explain to your people and that you keep follow-ups to a reasonable minimum (just the critical). Any volume of inquiries just compounds the problem.

A million thanks for your cooperation . . and remember—

> If you feel a little nervous
> When you find that daily service
> Is slower than expected
> Whether OK'd or rejected
> Keep in mind—it won't be long
> 'Til again—we're going strong

> Once the Transit strike is settled
> You'll no longer feel so nettled
> Your insureds will love you more
> We'll be "out front"—as before
> And our "service" will be back
> Like the subways—"on the track."

(Great letter? You're darned right!)

Appreciation from the president of a company for the excellent response to their annual blood bank appeal.

My Fellow Employees:

To be able to give is a blessing. Our company is indeed well blessed, for this year we have given 215 pints of blood for those who are less fortunate.

How can I thank you for your donations to this year's blood bank appeal? Not adequately, I know. But your real thanks is in the knowledge that you will have had a part in saving a life—returning a loved one to the family.

I am so proud of you all.

Humbly,

Thanks to an employee for an idea submitted.

Dear Mr. Morlan:

You know, that was an intriguing idea. I appreciate the thought that must have gone into it.

I've sent it on to the research people for evaluation—and when they've had a chance to study what you've suggested, you can be sure they'll be in touch with you.

Again, thanks—

Retirement

PRESIDENT OF COMPANY TO EMPLOYEE

Dear Jim:

They say a diplomat remembers birthdays but forgets ages. I must qualify (tho not through any conscious effort) to be diplomatic, because I had no idea until recently that you were about to retire.

While age may not come readily to mind, the achievements you'll leave behind you won't be forgotten by any of us. The years you've spent with the company have seen unparalleled growth in our business—growth that you helped make possible.

Change is a good thing, but it's a little sad when colleagues aren't with us any longer. Yet, you've certainly earned the time to relax and pursue your personal interests. You've given us many good years . . we're proud to have been associated with you.

Here's hoping that your new life with your family will be as pleasant for you as our association has been for me. All the best to you, and . . . keep in touch.

Sincerely,

TO A FRIEND

I hate to see you go, old buddy . . .

not that you haven't earned a long rest. You have but, all the same, without you the company won't be like it was.

But this is no time to be selfish. It's great that you have so many interests to look forward to, and such a wonderful family to share them with. I know how proud they are of you, and how happy that now you'll have so much more time with them.

I'll be passing through your new vacation spot in about two weeks, and I'll give a call then to pass on personal best wishes and congratulations. But for now, all the very best of luck, and here's to many happy years in the future.

You lucky stiff.

Cordially,

EMPLOYEE TO BOSS

Here you go . . .

after I'd gotten accustomed to your face . . . twisted in anger at some foolish mistake I'd made . . . you go and retire.

After I make you a present of a beautiful bull whip . . . you run off the target range.

After the entire department becomes a cohesive unit, working better than ever before . . . you leave.

Just because the company offers you a pension, you take it.

Boy, are you lucky. Sleeping late. Doing all the things you've only had vacations to do before.

I'm sure you'll take many memories with you. Please also take the thought that this place won't be the same without you. You'll be missed.

> Have a ball,

(Well, maybe *you* wouldn't write this . . . but don't you wish you could?)

Sales Records

CONGRATULATIONS ON BREAKING SALES QUOTA

Great Going, Chuck . . .

there's no greater feeling than when you go over that line. And knowing your sights were set on this goal, it proves how fine team effort can accomplish anything.

Keep it going—it's a swell habit to acquire. My best wishes for many top years in the future.

> Sincerely,

CONGRATULATIONS ON ACHIEVING MEMBERSHIP IN
GROUP OF TOP SALESMEN

Dear Miles:

Superlative achievement! There are no words that more perfectly describe your President's Council qualification.

My very heartiest congratulations on your fine, fine showing. And it's just one more step along your personal road of success—one of which we're all very proud.

Warmly,

CONGRATULATIONS ON
BEING NO. 1 COMPANY SALESMAN

My heartiest congratulations, Miles—

on being top salesman for our company in the entire country. This is just terrific, and not only a credit to you but to our entire organization.

A company's prestige and effectiveness is the direct result of the enthusiasm and follow-through of its men and women. You, Miles, are the perfect example of this positive attitude.

Cordially,

CONGRATULATIONS TO
A CONSISTENT TOP PRODUCER

Dear Jake:

You've certainly changed that old saying, "If at first you don't succeed, etc." In your case it should read, "If at first, and second, and third, and fourth you do succeed, try again."

I can't tell you how much pleasure it gives me to see you lead the field month after month. You're an excellent example, Jake, of dedication paying off.

Here's to next month—

Skoal!

Welcome

TO NEW STAFF MEMBER

Welcome, Mr. Edwards . . .

to Consolidated Steel. We're happy to have you with us.

You've joined us at a time of unprecedented growth in the American economy, in the steel industry—and in our company. The challenges and opportunities have never been greater . . the need for good people like you has never been greater.

We have a great future in front of us . . as individuals and as a company. I'm sure your intelligence and capabilities will play an important part.

Welcome,

Glad to have you with us, Mr. Jorge . . .

glad you selected Jensen as the place for your career; glad we're going to be working side-by-side.

In these first few weeks when things may seem a little foreign, or hectic, I sincerely hope you'll feel that my office door is always open . . and that you'll come on thru.

I'll look for you,

TO THE WIFE OF A NEW MEMBER

Dear Mrs. Edwards:

I hope you're as pleased as I that John decided to join Consolidated Steel. Naturally, I think it's a top-notch company and that we'll offer your husband a challenging and rewarding future.

But the most important thing is what John will be giving us. He is a highly intelligent man and will be a tremendous asset to us. Our business is complex, it is growing rapidly, and the future promises still greater growth and complexity.

John, and others like him, represent the foundation on which our growth will be based. Before many years, present management will pass on their responsibilities to others . . one of whom may very well be John. We will work together to see that he's ready.

During the next few weeks you'll see material about the company. I hope you enjoy reading it, for it will give you a comprehensive view of us and our goals.

And because both of you will be with us as we journey toward those goals, I say, "Welcome . . I'm very happy you're with us."

                                        Cordially,

Fund Raising

HAPPINESS FOR OVER 1200 CHILDREN

Mr. Kelly!

It's your fault!

Last year, just before Christmas, 26 of our girls returned ten minutes late from lunch—

Shopping bags full of dolls' clothing poured into the office, making the morning elevators even more hazardous than usual—

Our otherwise pristine filing cabinets were piled high with toys and games.

Two Assistant Directors were actually seen rolling a large multicolored beach ball up and down the hall while another was making for the Supply Closet with a Jigsaw Puzzle under his arm.

Our Supervisor became absolutely motherly—and total strangers smiled and spoke to each other—in fact there were general good spirits and fellowship throughout the Office.

Is this any way to run the Company?

You were also responsible for making last Christmas a happy one for over 1200 sick or underprivileged little boys and girls.

Is this any way to celebrate the Christmas Season?

We think so—Please do it again by sending your contribution for the 1967 Toy & Doll Drive to our Employee Association, in the enclosed envelope.

But remember—if our Campaign to help Santa is a success again this year—it will be because of you!

Gratefully,

HELP FOR MEN OVERSEAS

Dear Ed:

It's about "that time" again. Time to ask for help for the Red Cross Drive. I can imagine what you're saying. I've said it myself—one request for money after another. And just before tax time!

So writing this letter, when I first thought about it, seemed more difficult than my regular job of writing a legal brief.

In thinking of what might be said about Red Cross activities, all that came to mind were the same old coffee and doughnuts that were there thru tornadoes, hurricanes and fires. That made my letter more difficult. It had all been said.

Then last night, in the middle of a way-out TV show about aliens from outer space invading our country, a commercial came on. It was actual scenes from Vietnam showing the Red Cross—out on the battlefield—bringing blood to American soldiers. There were even scenes where the Red Cross trucks were under fire—and still getting through with that precious, life-saving blood.

It changed my mind, Ed, about writing you. Somehow after that, there weren't any questions in my own mind because for the small financial inconvenience to me, my donation might just help save one life over there. And that is worth more than any objection I can think of.

Will you think about your donation doing the same thing? And then, will you send me whatever you feel you'd like to give? An envelope is enclosed. But even more, the thanks of an unknowing army of men may also be enclosed.

Thanks,

THANK YOU FOR HELP ON
FUND RAISING CAMPAIGN

Dear Mike:

It wasn't easy . . fund raising never is . . but we did it. We went over our goal.

And a great deal of the credit goes to you for all those selfless hours you spent convincing people of the need for the hospital wing.

Will you thank your lovely wife, too? If she hadn't been selfless in letting you out each night, I'm not sure what we'd have done.

Appreciatively,

Without you, Carol . .

it never would have been such a success. We not only reached our goal, but went over . . with your help.

Thank you from the very deepest spot in my heart.

Fondly,

Recruiting—Sales personnel

ASKING FOR PROSPECTS FROM
A BUSINESSMAN IN SAME TOWN

Between ages 25 and 40—married

enthusiastic, ambitious, willing

presently employed—but restless

Does this description, Mr. Findhim . . .

fit anyone you know? If so, I'd like very much to talk with him about our organization.

Our Oshkosh branch is growing fast; our future looks real bright; and we're looking for men to fit into that future . . . men who are interested in being associated with some of the industry's top-flight representatives.

Of course, it would also put the icing on the cake, so to speak, if this chap you are thinking of was in good physical condition; made a good impression—appearance, voice, mannerisms; reliable; and had a good academic background.

Right now, while he's fresh in your mind, won't you jot his name and address on the bottom of this note and mail it to me in the enclosed envelope? You might be starting some young fellow on a rewarding career.

Thank you,

SEEKING CANDIDATES FROM
OTHER EXECUTIVES IN THE SAME INDUSTRY

Dear Paul:

Does your "cup runneth over"?

By that I mean do you know of some promising candidates
for your own sales staff . . . but just won't have room for
them for some time to come? If you do, I sure would
appreciate the chance to discuss the possibility of having
them come with our company.

I'm sure, Paul, I don't have to tell you the qualities for
which I'm looking. You have hired too many sales trainees
for me to do that. All I will say is that I have several
splendid openings right here in Missoula for good applicants
. . . preferably married and with a college education.

I certainly would be grateful if you would go over your list
of candidates and let me have a few names. Naturally, I will
say you recommended them to me—unless you prefer I
don't.

Who knows? Perhaps one good turn will deserve another
and I may be able to help you out one day. Let's give it a
try . . . what do you say?

Cordially,

WRITING A PROSPECTIVE CANDIDATE
WITHOUT LETTING HIM KNOW WHO
SUGGESTED HIS NAME

Dear Mr. Rave:

Someone thinks so highly of you . . .

he has recommended you as a likely candidate for one of
the positions I am going to have available soon. I wish I
could tell you who it was—but he preferred to remain anon-
ymous.

Our business here in Missoula has been increasing by such leaps and bounds that happily I am compelled to add to our sales staff. This means we have several splendid openings for capable, conscientious individuals who are anxious to build an outstanding career—with future earnings practically unlimited.

Possibly you have never considered selling life insurance. If so, I ask you to consider these two facts. Our industry is one of the fastest growing in the country today. Thus the chances for advancement in practically every capacity are far above average. And, it's one of the most respected and rewarding fields you could enter, since it affords so many opportunities to serve your fellow man.

But let's talk it over before reaching any decision. Could you stop by to see me Monday, about 5:30 P.M.? If for some reason you can't come in on that day, please give me a call and we can arrange an appointment for some other time.

I'll be looking forward to the pleasure of meeting you on Monday, the 10th.

Cordially,

12.

Saying "No"...it's how you say it that counts

Countless times in business it's necessary to say "NO" . . . many times by letter:

► when people ask for contributions,

► when they want you to advertise in special publications,

► when they return merchandise,

► when they ask you to donate prizes.

Some people have a talent for saying "no." Some, in fact, can tell us to go to hell . . . and have us *nod agreement* and thank them when they're done. How? A combination of honesty, personality, and, believe it or not, concern for the people they're writing to.

The first rule for a negative reply is to . . . BE POSITIVE! Has your correspondent made an honest request, in good faith? Does it involve rules or policies he couldn't know about or might have misunderstood? If you must say "no," can you offer an alternative? Is there a political reason why you should not send a routine turndown letter; such as the request that came from someone who has influence that could be used against you or your company?

Keep in mind that when people make requests, however routine they may seem to you, they generally are important to the people making them . . . sometimes extremely important. Consider the likely results of your letter before you send it . . . by the time you get unfavorable feedback, it's too late to consider what you *should have* done.

Here's an example of how not to say "no"—a letter from a large department store to a customer asking for a list of his bills for the past year.

> Dear Mr. Daley:
>
> The bills sent to you each month are itemized, and it is the customer's responsibility to keep these tabulations for reference. We can't be expected to act as bookkeeper for everyone who shops here.
>
> Sincerely,

Needless to say, Mr. Daley stopped shopping there. Had the letter been written this way, he might have remained a customer:

> This might disappoint you, Mr. Daley . . .
>
> but we aren't able to supply the information you requested about last year's bills. Our accounting system is set up to handle bills on a monthly basis, with itemization only for the previous month's purchases.
>
> We *can* supply the total amount you have spent each month in the past year, and those totals are enclosed. We don't, however, have any way of breaking them down.
>
> Again, I'm sorry we couldn't give you exactly what you wanted. But I hope this information will be helpful to you.
>
> Sincerely,

Here are other effective ways to say "no."

Turning down a request for contributions (*company*)

As you might imagine, Mr. Blasdel . . .

we get a great many requests each year for contributions to worthy causes such as yours. In an effort to do as much as we can, and in a fair manner, each year our contributions budget is allocated among various charities for the following year.

In addition, part of the budget is held aside for unanticipated requests like yours . . . but, unfortunately, that allocation too has already been exhausted for this year.

I'm sorry we can't help you right now. However, I'm keeping the literature you thoughtfully sent me, and when next year's budget is drawn up, we will certainly consider your organization.

Good luck with your activities.

Cordially,

Refusing to donate product

Dear Mr. Carter:

Thanks for thinking of "Walco," and for the kind invitation to participate in your rally next month. I wish we could take part.

Unfortunately, we have already exceeded our year's allocation of "Walclo" for such functions. You might think that since we manufacture it, we have an unlimited supply and could make an exception in your case. But I'm sure you realize one exception would be unfair to others we have to turn down. And to place no limit on the amount we give away would be impractical.

I'm sorry we aren't able to help . . . but, best wishes for a very successful rally.

Cordially,

Refusing a request for a refund

Dear Mr. Blue:

I sure wish I could say "send it back, we'll credit your account," but it just isn't possible.

You'll recall the order was made up specially for you . . and at the time we reminded you no refund was possible. We simply have no other outlet for the merchandise.

But all may not be lost. Several retailers in this area use similar items, and I've enclosed their names and addresses. Perhaps one of them would be interested in buying the merchandise from you. Also, if we have any future order for such merchandise, you can be sure we'll check you to see if yours is still available.

Sorry we can't do better for you. I hope you'll be successful in finding a customer among those we've suggested.

Cordially,

Turning down a request for contributions (individual)

That, Mr. Jonas . . .

was a very interesting appeal, and I agree that your organization is indeed worthy.

It was gratifying then, to learn that the United Fund allocates a part of its proceeds to your cause . . . gratifying because each year I make a substantial contribution to the United Fund rather than several smaller ones to individual organizations. A part of that contribution will be, or has already been sent to you through the United Fund.

I admire the good work you and your people are doing. Keep it up!

Sincerely,

Cancer Research, Phil . . .

is already one of my charities—mainly because it struck very close just two years ago.

My boss, who was only 49, died of cancer within one week of finding he had it. In his memory our department established a Memorial Fund at his college for research in this field. And twice a year, I make a pledged contribution.

My commitment, personally, is there, Phil. I'm sure you'll understand. And, of course, our Company makes one annual contribution to the national fund.

Sincerely,

Refusing an insurance claim

Dear Mrs. Wells:

I certainly hope Steven is recovering nicely from his recent illness. No matter what age children are, our concern as parents never lessens.

Actually, Mrs. Wells, your son is no longer covered by your policy. You probably had forgotten that once a child finishes school, your insurance covers him only until he reaches age 19. Since Steven is out of school and was 19 his last birthday . . we don't have the kind of news I know you hoped for.

May I make a suggestion? Before any more time passes . . or another illness strikes . . why not consider a policy for Steven himself? We'd be more than happy to help him select one that will be best suited for his present . . and future . . needs.

Sincerely,

cc: Mr. Agent

Turning down applicant for a job (person who almost qualifies)

Dear Mr. Finley:

We appreciate your interest in Acme Company and have carefully evaluated your application and qualifications.

Frankly, your qualifications are excellent, and that makes it doubly difficult to tell you that right now there isn't an available position to make the best use of them. Those that are open don't require your experience and wouldn't justify the salary you have a right to expect.

I know you hoped for better news, Mr. Finley, and I'm sorry we can't give it to you. But to offer you a job that is obviously not going to provide a challenge would be unfair.

Men with your experience and abilities are in demand throughout industry. You shouldn't have any trouble in locating a position in the near future. If I can be of any help to you in the meantime, please let me know.

Cordially,

Refusing job applicant (person not qualified)

I read your résumé, Mr. Angle . . .

with considerable interest. You've accomplished a great deal in your career.

If there were any openings in our company for someone with your qualifications, I'd certainly invite you to visit us. However, the jobs calling for your capabilities are invariably filled from within the company. All we could offer would be a trainee position, and I doubt you'd want to waste your time and experience starting all over again.

But I thank you for your interest, and wish you the best of luck in finding a new position.

Cordially,

Turning down a request to advertise

Dear Mr. Allen:

Normally we like to assist publications such as yours. Aside from our regularly scheduled advertising, which is set well in advance, we have a special fund for last minute local advertising.

Unfortunately, that fund has already been used up by the unusually large number of requests so far this year. I'm sure you can understand that it isn't possible to keep adding to that budget, no matter how small the amounts.

So, as much as we'd like to participate in your publication, it just isn't possible this year. But, if there's any other way we can be of help to you, I certainly hope you'll let me know.

Cordially,

There are other types of turndown letters you may have to write, but in them, as well as the ones you've just read, the techniques are the same:

►when saying "no," give enough reason so the reader will understand.

►if an alternative is possible, offer it.

►keep a positive attitude toward the person you're writing . . be polite and as gentle as possible. Don't offend or hurt if you can help it . . it won't do you or your company any good.

13.

Selling the sizzle...

To a certain extent, all letters are sales letters . . . whether you're selling a product, service, yourself, advice, point of view or trying to gain your reader's good will and understanding.

Let's confine ourselves here to letters that are specifically intended to sell a product or service. Certainly no other type letter has such a potentially high return on the investment that goes into it.

They're important. Why? Because sales build business. Face-to-face selling isn't always possible; the letter takes the place of a personal call . . . or paves the way for a personal call. And letters get to more people faster than door-to-door salesmen.

The objective of a sales letter, obviously, is to get your reader nodding in agreement so he'll act as you want him to. So he'll buy. Don't take a chance that he'll do as you want. No, *plan* it and *lead your reader* to the conclusion you want him to reach. Basically, this involves four steps:

(1) Capture his attention right away, with your first words.

(2) Build his desire for what you offer . . . build a need and then show that what you have will satisfy that need.

You're not selling soap; you're selling cleanliness, good smells and sex appeal.

You're not selling skin medicine; you're selling clear skin that will attract the opposite sex.

You're not selling food; you're selling solid nourishment for the family, convenience for the housewife, superb quality and taste.

(3) Once you've built his interest and defined his need, present enough facts to convince the reader that your product or service is just the thing he wants. He must be motivated to act as you want him to.

(4) End your letter with a call to action. Don't write merely that he'll enjoy your product. Tell him to act quickly, while the offer lasts, or before the product is sold out, or before his friends beat him to it.

In short, don't stop with implying action . . . state exactly what you want the reader to do, and when you want him to do it.

Openings that gain attention

Almost any device will do . . . ask a question, tell a story (provided it's a short story—very short), make a statement that will startle the reader, arouse his curiosity, offer something free.

A salesman selling pool covers wrote:

> Is your swim pool a danger, Mr. Aqua?

> (Startling? Sure is.)

The new car models came out, and a salesman wrote:

> We'll supply the gas, free, Mr. Ponty.

> (Free offer.)

A local boutique wrote the women in town:

> Do other women envy your clothes, Mrs. Schwab?

> (What a question!)

The Hometown Travel Agency wrote:

> Do grass skirts interest you, Mr. Raabe?

> (No comment!)

Building desire

People don't buy products for what they are . . . they buy for what the product will do for them.

Will it slake their thirst? . . . fulfill a hunger? . . . make them rich? . . . or popular? . . . or intelligent? . . . attractive to that guy, that gal?

Will it make life easy? . . . save them time? . . . give them a great reputation? . . . preserve their health? . . . keep them safe? . . . protect them from trouble?

When you're selling something, build up those aspects of your product that will heighten a desire—make an emotional appeal to your reader.

Converting desire to conviction

When you're aiming for a kiss, don't settle for a handshake!

Once the desire is identified in your reader, present enough facts to convince him your product will do all he wants it to do. Don't expect the reader to have blind faith in you or what you offer. *Convince him*—present facts that will prod him to that conclusion.

Naturally this means you should know all there is to know about the product. Use it yourself—find out what the attractive features are and write about them. You can't convince others unless you're convinced first!

Now that you've gained attention with your opening, we'll add a paragraph convincing the reader your product should interest him:

(*pool cover*)

> Our pool cover will give you peace of mind. No child can possibly be hurt if, at the end of the season, you put one of our covers on and fasten it to the sides of the pool.

> I can vouch for its strength, because I have walked across the one which covers my own pool.

(*new car*)

> Don't just take our word for the easy steering, comfortable driving and cool air conditioning of our new model car. To say nothing of the 7 high-fashion colors!

(*beautiful gown*)

> If you want to be the most talked about, admired and envied woman in your town, you should be wearing our beautiful

gowns. They are one-of-a-kind, designed just for you. Even copycats won't be able to, now.

(*Hawaiian sounds*)

Maybe you can't get to Hawaii this year. But wouldn't you like to enjoy the sound of the surf breaking on the sand, the swish of palm trees blowing in the soft breeze, the rustle of grass skirts to beautiful Hawaiian ukuleles?

Calling for action

Most people won't act unless you give them a good reason.

The last part of a sales letter is the place where they'll slow down. The tendency is to put the letter aside and say, "I'll do it tomorrow"—and in those cases, tomorrow rarely comes. Your problem in sales letters is to get them to act *right away*.

How? Try a limited time or limited quantity offer; or a money-back guarantee; or a free trial; a discount for immediate orders; offer credit.

Say you'll send the product unless you are told not to (thereby taking advantage of the human impulse to do nothing): offer a bonus for immediate action.

Let's write a call to action for each of the above paragraphs:

(*pool cover*)

And, Mr. Aqua, if you buy your pool cover before August 30, we will also give you—free of charge—a gallon of liquid chlorine.

Wednesday evening, I'll phone to see when it would be convenient for me to come by and show you the protection you'll be buying.

(*new car*)

Come in and drive it. And, Mr. Ponty, we'd be delighted to have you bring your wife and children to take the ride with you.

I've set aside Sunday at 2:00 P.M. for your test drive. I'm personally looking forward to showing you the latest in automobiles.

(*beautiful gown*)

And for the next two months, only, each gown you have made, Mrs. Schwab, will contain a label reading—

"Made exclusively for Mrs. Schwab."

Exciting? Yes, it is. Won't you try to stop in the shop. We'd like to get started on *your* gown.

(*Hawaiian sounds*)

Send today for all those wonderful sounds. They're in our latest album of Hawaiian music.

An envelope is enclosed. Just put your $5.95 check in it, send it to me . . then sit back with a cool papaya cocktail and plan on relaxing elegantly. The record will arrive shortly.

And here are the complete letters . . . letters that sell!

(*pool cover*)

Is your swim pool a danger, Mr. Aqua?

Our pool cover will give you peace of mind. No child can possibly be hurt if, at the end of the season, you put one of our covers on and fasten it to the sides of the pool.

I can vouch for its strength, because I have walked across the one which covers my own pool.

And, Mr. Aqua, if you buy your pool cover before August 30, we will also give you—free of charge—a gallon of liquid chlorine.

Wednesday evening, I'll phone to see when it would be convenient for me to come by and show you the protection you'll be buying.

Thank you,

(*new car*)

We'll supply the gas, free, Mr. Ponty—

Don't just take our word for the easy steering, comfortable driving and cool air conditioning of our new model car. To say nothing of the 7 high-fashion colors!

Come in and drive it. And, Mr. Ponty, we'd be delighted to have you bring your wife and children to take the ride with you.

I've set aside Sunday at 2:00 P.M. for your test drive. I'm personally looking forward to showing you the latest in automobiles.

Happy Driving!

(*beautiful gown*)

Do other women envy your clothes, Mrs. Schwab?

If you want to be the most talked about, admired and envied woman in your town, you should be wearing our beautiful gowns. They are one-of-a-kind, designed just for you. Even copycats won't be able to, now.

And for the next two months, only, each gown you have made, Mrs. Schwab, will contain a label reading—

"Made exclusively for Mrs. Schwab."

Exciting? Yes, it is. Won't you try to stop in the shop.
We'd like to get started on *your* gown.

Make it soon—

(Hawaiian sounds)

Do grass skirts interest you, Mr. Raabe?

Maybe you can't get to Hawaii this year. But wouldn't
you like to enjoy the sound of the surf breaking on the
sand, the swish of palm trees blowing in the soft breeze, the
rustle of grass skirts to beautiful Hawaiian ukuleles?

Send today for all those wonderful sounds. They're in our
latest album of Hawaiian music.

An envelope is enclosed. Just put your $5.95 check in it,
send it to me . . . then sit back with a cool papaya cock-
tail and plan on relaxing elegantly. The record will arrive
shortly.

Aloha . .

On the following pages are examples of letters that sell . . .

not the book . . but the knowledge
not the beauty aid . . but the beauty
not the policy . . but the protection
not the product . . but the pride

Selling knowledge

Many people these days, Mr. Healy . . .

make no distinction between knowledge and intelligence.
But there is a difference. Intelligence is given us at birth.

Knowledge is gained over the years. Knowledge has to be worked for . . it has to be earned.

Now there is a weekly magazine designed specially for those who are willing to take the time necessary to remain in touch with the things going on around them; who want to have a comprehensive knowledge of the environment surrounding them. That magazine is *The Argus*.

The Argus is staffed by leading experts in over 100 different disciplines ranging from movies to religion to Far Eastern affairs. These experts are supported by a field reporting staff located all over the world. Together they search out, analyze, report and interpret for our readers the events in the news —and many events not generally in the news.

Our readers are among the best informed anywhere. They make a distinction between intelligence and knowledge.

I'm sure you do, too. And that's why I think you'll want to return the enclosed card quickly so that your subscription to *The Argus* can start with the next issue.

Happy reading . .

Selling beauty

Isn't the sun wonderful, Mrs. Wilson?

Warm and soothing, relaxing and peaceful.

But isn't it awful to the skin and hair?

Don't give it another thought. Now there's a way to protect your skin and hair from the damage the sun does to them . . . a way to keep your skin soft, smooth and moist, your hair glistening, alive and soft to the touch . . . and your time in the sun carefree.

BEAUTYAID shampoo is the first product ever designed for use on the body *and* on the hair. It is a special formula whose ingredients replace the natural oils the sun removes . . . keeping you lovely no matter what the sun and wind conspire to do.

An added feature is that except in cases of severe sunburn, BEAUTYAID will prevent peeling. That means the tan you work so hard to get will not flake and peel and be unsightly.

And the scents built into BEAUTYAID are so special that perfume is practically unnecessary.

BEAUTYAID is rapidly becoming the rage of women throughout the country. In fact, in your town, we know over thirty attractive women who are using it already. Don't you owe it to yourself to use the best product of its kind available?

Why not visit your drugstore this week and pick up a bottle of BEAUTYAID. It's on sale. After you've used it once, you'll wonder how you lived without it . . . and so will "he."

                                                        Happy sunning,

Selling protection

"All of a sudden the car swerved, pulled to the left, out into the traffic. I pulled at the wheel but the car was impossible to control. Finally I hit the guard rail and stopped. The car's a mess. But, thank God, no one was killed. The officer said I had a blowout."

That, Mr. Jones . .

is a direct quote from a young wife and mother who was very lucky last week. No one was killed, but they might have been. Do you trust your family's safety to luck? Are you sure you won't have a blowout? If your wife has one, will she be lucky?

Why take the chance? Luck is fickle . . Firestrong tires aren't. They can be trusted with your family's lives.

Shouldn't you get some today? I'm here at the store every day—and very glad to help.

Most sincerely,

What would happen, Dr. Tuck . . .

if you were stricken ill tomorrow and couldn't practice? Perhaps better than anyone, you, as a doctor know the suddenness with which illness can strike, and the misery and financial hardships it can cause.

In your case, the inconvenience and financial worries could be especially great. Who would pay the rent for your office, the salaries of your staff, the living expenses for your family? As an independent businessman, you more than most would suffer.

But suffering can be avoided . . not the suffering of illness . . the financial suffering that is the handmaiden of illness.

As a doctor and self-employed professional man, you qualify for a specially designed program that can completely remove the possibility that sickness or accident could be a financial nightmare. This program will take over, if you are unable to practice, where you left off . . providing your family with an income to meet its needs.

You are very busy, I know, but I honestly feel consideration of this program is worth the few minutes of your valuable time it will take me to explain it. And I do promise to be brief and to the point.

Would before or after office hours be more convenient for you? May I suggest Wednesday, August 22—and leave the time up to you. I'll phone your secretary several days before, and she can let me know your choice.

Thanks so much,

P.S. If you prefer, I'd be happy to meet with your account-ant or lawyer to show them the merits of the program, if you are unable to break away.

Selling pride

It's hard to keep up, Mr. Wales . . .

with all the activity taking place in the electrical field. New devices, new methods are popping up all the time.

I know you pride yourself on carrying the latest available equipment—only the best for your customers. So, I thought it would be beneficial to you if you could see some brand new products Acme Electric has just introduced.

These products are revolutionary, and will make a healthy contribution to your business and your reputation as the best electrical contractor in the area.

Would next Tuesday at 2 P.M. be OK for me to drop by? I'll call your secretary to confirm the time. And, I think you'll agree it will be time well spent.

Until Tuesday . . .

Have you ever had the experience, Mr. Halsted . . .

of working night and day on your company's Annual Re-port and then had it come off the press with a paragraph missing? What do you tell the president? That you didn't make the mistake, the printer did? Or the artist?

It shouldn't be necessary to make any explanations. Such errors should never happen. And they don't when the outside suppliers you work with take as much pride in your work as you do.

We, at Acme Inc., do take pride in *your* work. Beginning with the initial concept of the printed piece, our artists execute a design specifically to meet your objectives—and we follow it through printing and delivery to you.

Because we are a fully integrated graphics design and printing company, responsibility for your work is centralized in one place. Art doesn't get lost on the way to the printer . . type isn't misplaced on the way to the artist. Each job is done as it should be—properly. The first time.

We have grown because of people like you who take pride in their work, and appreciate expert assistance from first-rate designers and printers. We are successful because we deliver the best work around . . and with all paragraphs in place.

I'm enclosing samples of recently completed jobs for you to look at. After you've read them, perhaps you'll ask your secretary to set aside a few minutes next week for us to chat about what we can do to help you! I'll phone her in a few days to get the date.

Believe me, Mr. Halsted, for a man who won't settle for less than the best, it's a worthwhile few minutes.

Thank you for listening,

Remember . . . as Elmer Wheeler said: "Don't sell the steak—sell the sizzle."

14.

Unaccustomed as I am...

You're right! This is a chapter dedicated to the art of preparing a speech or talk, as we prefer. And how does it fit into a book on letterwriting? Very easily.

If you can write a good letter, you can put together a good talk. They're very similar. Both must have:

.. a solid beginning to set the stage and gain attention for what comes later;

.. a middle in which you develop your points;

.. an ending in which you sum up and make a lasting impression on your audience.

But a talk offers something a letter doesn't. It's verbal. You have the advantage of your hands, facial expressions, the tone of your voice. In this book, we've tried to show the difference it can make when your letter is conversational. That same difference applies when you give a speech . . . so give a "talk."

Just as you do with letters:

.. know the main purpose of your talk—and if there's a second purpose, know that too!

.. firmly fix in mind the approach you want to take—serious, mysterious, humorous, and, as in letterwriting—use humor cautiously!

.. be clear on what you want your listeners to know—or you might ramble all over the place.

.. decide if there is any way the listener can benefit from what you have to say—and if so, how.

.. know exactly the thought you want to leave in your audience's mind—and plan it for your close.

When you're preparing a talk:

Be sure the topic is close to your heart. Don't ever get put into the position of talking on a subject with which you're not 100% familiar.

Dale Carnegie puts it this way: "Talk about something you have earned the right to talk about through long study or experience."

Want to give your talk. Think positively about your audience . . . be anxious to please them. Give them every benefit of the doubt—believe they are anxious to hear what you have to say.

Feel strongly about the message you have to give—be emphatic and dynamic in your delivery. Make your listeners feel as you do about your subject.

Write it yourself. No one thinks and speaks as you do. If you prepare your own material it will suit you . . . it will sound natural.

Plan. Before you ever jot down a sentence, make notes of the points you want to make—the important facts you must include—anything humorous to lighten your message.

Get off to a fast, interesting start. Let's pretend you've been asked to talk about your favorite car. You could begin by saying—

I've been asked to speak to you about my favorite car. It is the Superduper Sport.

(10 members of the audience sit back, yawn and say "wonder how long this will take. Sounds pretty dull.")

But if you stood up and said—

Let me tell you about the best doggone car on the market —except for Bolt #23.

Now if we'd been writing a letter about the subject, we might have started it—

Let me tell you, Joe . . .

about the best darned car on the market. And also about Bolt #23.

Got the picture? See the similarity between letters and talks?

Give examples of what you mean. Give facts, reasons, use exhibits. If you're going to talk about the best car on the market, tell your audience why—make them believe it is the best by giving facts.

30 miles to the gallon isn't bad, right? Well, that's what my car gives me.

Bolt #23 is important because it's the bolt that holds the front wheel in place.

or

Hold up Bolt #23!

Now you're talking your listeners' language . . examples like that are easily understood!

Put conversation into your talk. Instead of simply saying the fellow in the showroom was a good salesman, try . .

> The salesman turned from me right to my wife and said, "What color upholstery would compliment your wardrobe most, Mrs. Speiker?" Wasn't he the smooth one!

People love to listen to dialogue. It breaks up a monologue of statements of fact . . just as in letters quotations interrupt the monotony of long paragraphs or explanations.

End with a bang. Leave your audience with a lasting impression . . give them something to take away with them. Comedians say, "Leave your audience laughing." A speaker should "leave his audience remembering."

Sticking with our story on the best car—you set your listeners on the edge of their chairs with your opening—the mysterious Bolt #23.

You've stayed clear of it throughout your talk—except one small fact about what it does. And now you're ready to close. Can't you see each fella sitting, waiting to see what happened to Bolt #23?

And so you close—

> Well, that's my story . . why in my book there just isn't any car like the Superduper Sport. I'd recommend it to all of you.

> Oh yes, one suggestion. Before you leave the showroom, check Bolt #23. On my car—it was missing!

What a finish! You've held their attention—and then closed with a clincher. You've done one other thing—you've made them want more—'cause now, they're dying to hear all about that missing Bolt.

Your talk won't be forgotten. Just as in letterwriting, keep your audience with you from the beginning to the end.

15.

There are letters...
and there are letters

By now you've probably figured out that many letters can be categorized . . . collection, sales, follow-up. There are also letters that don't fit any category. They just stop you cold because they're so good. They're letters with a message.

The man who says "show me a sign" will probably never learn to write this sort of letter. They are the product of great imagination and the willingness to open up on paper and show the world what's under your skin . . . and under your skull.

The best description of these letters is the letters themselves. So we've put in a few for you to read. It is devoutly to be wished that every letter ever written could be as good. But then, perfection might get dull.

INSPIRATION . . . *to a Jew from a Christian*

Dear Larry:

Your Father and Mother invited Mrs. McCarthy and me to your Bar Mitzvah, and although we are unable to attend, we want to offer you our sincerest congratulations on achieving this hallmark in your life.

As Christians, the best way we know of sending our good wishes is through prayer . . prayer that is perhaps formally different from yours—but prayer offered to the same loving God. Our priest and friend, Father Burke, will join us in prayer for your special intention on the day of your Bar Mitzvah.

As a man and a Jew, you will touch many people in your life who are of another faith. If a dialogue can be established, you'll find that the differences are of little meaning. Life's purpose—yours, ours, and your parents—must surely include an attempt to understand and respect each other's beliefs.

Dominus vobiscum!

PRIDE . . . *from the President of the Board of Directors to the young athletes of his church and school*

How do I put into words the pride your Board of Directors feels in its young men who have earned the right to test their skills and prove themselves among the toughest of competition?

Is congratulations enough? It hardly seems so.

To be one of the top 8 contenders in our nation on the basketball court is no small accomplishment—it is a great feat.

Not everyone is so fortunate as to have the opportunity to prove to himself—and his contemporaries—how well he is prepared to meet life's many challenges with its share of trials and triumphs. And you will prove it—of that we are sure.

And we are also very happy that our long-sought goal—a gymnasium of our own—is close to being realized. All the support each of us is able to give to this project will help speed the day when it can be fully utilized.

May God move many interested persons to share in our goal, and thereby bless thousands of young lives for years to come.

AFFECTION . . . *A father tells the Dean of Freshmen at Notre Dame about his son who has just entered the University.*

We've been putting this letter together for nearly a month now, Dean Burke . . . ever since you told us at orientation that we could expect an inquiry from you, asking parents to help you know more about their boys . . . *your* boys now.

Steve is a young man who seemed to grow slowly physically and in maturity. Then, suddenly, he acquired both in a single year . . . principally because he acquired responsibilities—a job; he earned a driver's license; he began to like a girl. He became a high school senior and, while nearly all his critical academic work had already been completed, he knew it would be important for him to maintain his good academic standing. Whatever Steve earned, he wanted to be sure he earned it on his own. And he did. He led his class.

He was president of the chorus, stalwart in the band and orchestra, member of the Honor Society and Leaders Club. He tried his hand at debating and dramatics. He played Frosh football (he weighed 85 pounds then); he played soccer two years, ran cross-country and the two-mile. And he can tell you football, basketball, baseball and hockey players by number and name.

When he finally had to make a choice between sports and music, he chose music—because he felt he contributed more there and that the music groups relied on him.

Steve gravitated naturally toward diversity of interests. We didn't urge it on him—but neither did we discourage it . . . because such diversity provides youngsters (and adults too) with the best possible opportunity to understand their fellow men in all their pursuits.

Steve has a great love for people—an empathy with nearly everyone he meets. He is equally comfortable with the waitress or the cook in the restaurant . . . or with the rough-talking laborer in the sheet metal shop . . . or with the teacher who loves poetry . . . or another who loves music.

He enjoys art museums . . . but if you look in his trunk, you will find there his caricature of Snoopy.

He can be absorbed in Hemingway or Salinger . . . but he is also delighted by Peanuts in the comic strip, and the first column he turns to in the newspapers is Jimmy Cannon on the sports page.

He enjoys Mozart and Bach, Bernstein and Copland . . . but he is enthralled also by Barbra Streisand, the Beatles and Peter, Paul and Mary.

Is this contrast or balance? Perhaps it's simply great empathy.

He is energetic, inquisitive, idealistic, loyal. He is a critical reader, a critical listener. He is articulate (verbally and in writing). He is thoughtful . . . yet a typically impatient brother with his sisters, and a typically impatient son with his parents.

His teachers have had a great and positive influence on him. And he, in turn, has influenced them.

And he's stubborn. Sometimes too stubborn to be aware of his own physical exhaustion.

But you and your staff will be watching, won't you.

Cordially,

HUMOR . . . *greatest reply to a collection letter ever written*

Dear Deputy Collector:

This is to inform you (for the third time) that I made every effort to persuade Mr. Lee Zimmerman to meet his obligation to the City of New York—especially the retail sales tax. And, for the third time he refused to listen to me.

The first time you requested the tax receipt, Mr. Zimmerman was dead . . . He was dead the second time you wrote . . . He is still dead.

But don't despair. Try me again when the next installment is due. Or better still, run down to Maspeth Cemetery, plot three, path 33 and see if you can't persuade him to see your side of it.

Meanwhile, keep in touch. I get so little mail these days.

Sincerely,

APPRECIATION . . . *from an ex-secretary*

How can I thank you . . .

for the many things you have taught me—not only about business but about life itself. I think because of you, I am now a better person.

I enjoyed being your secretary. But even more, I enjoyed having you for my friend. Thank you for *everything!*

I only hope that my feather will always be the tallest one you will wear in your hat!

Thanks again,

PASSING OF THE REINS . . .

Dear Marjane:

The frame is beginning to feel the strain. Not only that, I have so many personal things I would like to do before turning in my uniform for keeps, and time is running out.

This is a long way around of saying that I wish to resign as Correspondence Consultant to MONY as of the end of this year.

I must admit, Marjane, that after the most pleasant relationship with all of you over the past 24 years, it does bring a slight lump to my throat to write this letter. But I know you are more than well qualified to carry on the program started way back in 1943, and I am confident that you will make a grand success of it.

I owe so much to so many of you. For the splendid co-operation and backing I have had—the rich and sometimes exciting experiences—and the always wonderful associations with so many grand people. I am taking with me a treasure house of marvelous memories.

And you have added so much to that store, Marjane. I can't begin to tell you how much I have enjoyed working with you and discovering what a truly fine person you are. And such a fine pupil. Management should have no qualms in turning over the reins to you, and I am proud to have such a capable successor.

My very best wishes to all of you in the years that lie ahead.

Most sincerely,

Richard H. Morris

FAITH . . . *for the children of the world—*

Is there a Santa Claus?

Virginia, your little friends are wrong. They have been affected by the skepticism of a skeptical age. They do not believe except they see. They think that nothing can be which is not comprehensible by their little minds. All minds, Virginia, whether they be men's or children's, are little. In this great universe of ours, man is a mere insect, an ant, in his intellect, as compared with the boundless world about him, as measured by the intelligence capable of grasping the whole truth and knowledge.

Yes, Virginia, there is a Santa Claus. He exists as certainly as love and generosity and devotion exist, and you know that they abound and give to your life its highest beauty and joy. Alas! how dreary would be the world if there were no Santa Claus! It would be as dreary as if there were no Virginias. There would be no childlike faith, then no poetry, no romance to make tolerable this existence. We should have no enjoyment, except in sense and sight. The external light with which childhood fills the world would be extinguished.

Not believe in Santa Claus! You might as well not believe in fairies! You might get your papa to hire men to watch in all the chimneys on Christmas Eve to catch Santa Claus, but even if they did not see Santa Claus coming down, what would that prove? Nobody sees Santa Claus, but that is no sign that there is no Santa Claus. The most real things in the world are those that neither children nor men can see. Did you ever see fairies dancing on the lawn? Of course not, but that's no proof that they are not there. Nobody can conceive or imagine all the wonders there are unseen and unseeable in the world.

You tear apart the baby's rattle and see what makes the noise inside, but there is a veil covering the unseen world which not the strongest man, not even the united strength of all the strongest men that ever lived, could tear apart. Only faith, fancy, poetry, love, romance, can push aside that curtain and view—and picture the supernal beauty and glory beyond. Is it all real? Ah, Virginia, in all this world there is nothing else real and abiding.

No Santa Claus! Thank God he lives, and he lives forever. A thousand years from now, Virginia, nay, ten times ten thousand years from now, he will continue to make glad the heart of childhood.

16.

Tidbits of information for that "Gal Friday"

Do you know what being a "Gal Friday" means?

You've heard the saying, "Behind every successful man there's a woman." Well, we think "Behind every successful man there's a Gal Friday!" And that means you're an ultra-important part of your boss's business life.

You're . . .

►his personal public relations agent

►his loyal subject

►his understanding teammate

►his buffer against the public

►his sounding board

►his keeper-of-secrets

►his "mother hen"

►his secretary

►indispensable

And because you are all these things, whatever your boss knows, you should know something of; whatever he reads, you should read; whatever he studies, you should study.

And since he's been reading this book, you have, too. So we're including some questions that came up in talking with gals like you about material for this book. (We're also including the answers!)

Abbreviations

Q: When is it proper to abbreviate names and places?

Names—NEVER. You can't impress someone if you haven't even time to write out his name!

Abbreviating places, such as states, may be proper—but it isn't preferable.

Q: Is it all right to abbreviate a person's title?

Not if you're interested in his good will.

Complimentary Close

Q: Is it necessary to use "Sincerely" or "Cordially" at all times?

Certainly not! In fact, throughout this book there is little use of either word. Today's business letter must be out of the ordinary from start to close to get attention . . . and these words show very little imagination.

Why not try—

"Hopefully" when you want something
"Appreciatively" when someone has done something
"Regretfully" when you can't do something

"Apologetically" when you're sorry
"Gratefully" as an alternate for "appreciatively"
"Thank you" when all you want to say is "thanks"

and any other interesting, suitable phrase.

Dictation

Q: When taking dictation, is it proper to interrupt if Mr. Boss is dictating too fast?

Not only proper—a "must"! You'll find he won't mind your question half as much as he'll mind getting an incorrect transcript.

Q: Is it necessary for him to dictate punctuation and paragraphing?

That depends on you. If he can rely on you to do this properly, it isn't necessary. But if there is the slightest doubt in your own mind about how well you will do it, let him dictate.

Q: If the wording, grammar or punctuation Mr. Boss dictates doesn't sound correct, may I change it?

This should be governed entirely by your boss's wish. Some bosses will insist you do—others prefer you don't. We suggest when you first work with a man, you ask his preference.

Grammar

Q: Are contractions acceptable?

Since today's style of writing is becoming more and more conversational, contractions are becoming more and more popular. They do add a more informal touch.

Q: Is it permissible to split an infinitive?

Most letter-writing authorities agree it is . . . if it makes your letter sound more natural.

Q: Should every sentence have a subject and predicate?

It isn't a complete sentence without them. But when you are breaking up a lengthy sentence having several ideas . . . you may break this rule and use an incomplete sentence for comfort and ease of reading. For example:

Will you please send us your policy? Also the completed change of beneficiary form.

Q: How long should a sentence be? A paragraph?

There's no set rule—but if a sentence runs over twenty words, and a paragraph over ten lines, the reader has difficulty following your train of thought. Long sentences and paragraphs even *look* hard to read. You weary your reader before he starts.

Q: If your boss doesn't tell you, how can you decide when to start a new paragraph?

When one thought changes to another. However, there may be times when the discussion of one thought gets too lengthy . . . so you'll need to break it into more than one paragraph.

Q: How can I emphasize words in a letter?

By underscore . . . or solid caps. Just a word of caution— don't use either too often or the emphasis is lost entirely.

Postscripts

Q: Is a postscript proper?

Not only proper . . . but a decided plus. While the postscript originally meant an afterthought, today it's a well-planned beforethought.

If you really want something to stand out . . . to emphasize a point . . . a postscript is the place.

Punctuation

Q: Are we using fewer commas today?

Yes. Just don't carry it too far. Commas can make a sentence easier to read.

Q: Is the semicolon becoming obsolete?

To an extent. More and more people are using short sentences—or separating phrases with dots . . . or dashes—

Q: Should a phrase such as "Will you please sign this receipt" be followed by a question mark?

No. Actually you're making a request, not asking a question.

Reference Line

Q: When should I use a reference line, i.e., "Account #23456—J. Jones" above the body of a letter?

Any time it is necessary to refer to previous correspondence, account numbers, or even subjects. It makes identification easier . . . and avoids cluttering up the body of your letter.

Q: Is it necessary to use "re" or "subject" before the reference line?

No. Its position makes that obvious.

Salutations

Q: If addressing a letter to a corporation, which salutation should be used, "Dear Sir" or "Gentlemen"?

"Gentlemen" is correct since a company is not an individual.

In fact, never use "Dear Sir." If you know the person to whom you're writing is a male—you must know his name . . . so use it.

Q: May I omit a salutation?

Yes, if you use the Simplified Form of letter. Not only is the salutation omitted, but also the complimentary close.

However, our own personal opinion is that it makes the letter very cold.

Q: When should I use "Attention: Mr. So-and-So"?

Never. As long as you have the name of any individual in a company, your letter should be addressed to him.

Q: Is there such a thing as a "headline salutation"?

You bet . . . and throughout this book you'll find many of them—

Have you forgotten, Mr. Pabehind . . .

Are you aware, Mr. Dawson . . .

How is Susan, Mrs. Kay?

These are all "headline salutations"—they're becoming more and more the most up-to-date way to open letters. The form serves several purposes:

▶gets letter off to a fast start

▶eliminates "dear," a gratuitous word that seldom applies

▶immediately grabs the reader's attention

If you use these salutations, keep several points in mind— or they lose their effect:

Make the salutation about half as long as your second line.

Yes, Mr. Jones . . . .

we did order your new Bonneville. It should be in by next Saturday.

Be sure the reader's name is at the end of the first line; never carry it to a second line.

Thank heaven, Mr. Jones . . .

for good hospitals and doctors. But they are expensive, aren't they?

Leave two spaces between the salutation and your next line.

Your second line should continue the thought of the first. So don't capitalize the first word on the second line—and don't indent it.

My reaction, Mr. Jones . .

would have been the same as yours. But the white top on the dark green body makes it a good-looking convertible.

When you use a headline salutation, put the name and address at the bottom—that's called the Official Style letter form.

Since this is an unusual type of salutation, make your complimentary close unusual also. When appropriate, use those on the second page of this chapter.

Signatures

Q: When a woman writes a letter should she indicate "Miss" or "Mrs"?

If she signs her name using initials—

J. M. Smith

she must also show either (Miss) or (Mrs.)

If she signs her full first name—

Jane M. Smith

she need only indicate if she is (Mrs.)

Q: If a person signs his—or her—name "M. Martinez," how do I address him—or her?

Rather than make an embarrassing mistake, we've done things like—

Forgive me, M. Martinez . . .

for addressing you so personally. But from your note I wasn't sure whether to address you Mr., Miss or Mrs.

Q: Should the name of the person dictating the letter be typed under his signature?

Only if he is not using letterhead that gives his name. But if the letterhead does not show his name . . . type it under the complimentary close.

206 The Modern Business Letter Writer's Manual

Q: Is it all right to sign a letter with the boss's signature if he is away?

Yes . . . if he permits it. But be sure to note that it was signed in his absence—otherwise, it might appear he was too indifferent to sign it himself.

Q: Should a personal note concerning family or an event be included in a business letter? If so—where?

The beginning, the end, or a postscript . . . wherever it logically fits. However, under no circumstances include a message of sympathy in a business letter.

Q: Is it proper to write a reply on the bottom of a letter and return it?

We don't advocate this—but it is being done as a timesaver.

But there is one absolute "no." If you receive a letter of congratulations, you'd be rude to think so little of the sender that you return his applause.

Style

Q: How can I decide which style to use—block, full block, semiblock, indented, official or simplified?

First—ask Mr. Boss for his preference.

Block is rapidly becoming the #1 choice. It looks compact . . . spaces more evenly . . . takes less typing time . . . makes a letter look easier to read.

Our #1 choice is a combination of the block and official —blocked paragraphs but with name and address at the bottom.

Terminology

Q: Is it always necessary to use the word "company" when referring to our own organization?

No. It sounds much more natural to say "we," "us," "our." Or alternate among "company," "we" and the company name.

Q: Is it okay to start a paragraph with the personal pronoun "I"?

Of course—just don't overuse it, or your reader will feel you're an egotist.

Q: If I start with "Thank you," may I close with the same phrase?

It sure doesn't show much imagination!

Q: Is it ever proper to use "I" when writing in the name of the company?

Certainly . . . proper and often better than "we." Haven't you often felt ridiculous writing

We were happy to receive your note.

Can't you see every employee of the company happy about receiving that note? It's more sense to say

I was happy to receive your note.

I'll be anxious to have your decision.

Please fill out the enclosed application and return it to me.

Typing

Q: Is it necessary to type an inside address on a printed form letter?

When the letter is part of an over-all mailing, and no individual record is needed, the inside address may be omitted.

Q: In a 2- or 3-page letter, should I type some identification at the top of all pages after the first?

Yes. In case they become separated, it's good to have at least the recipient's name on each page.

Q: In a short note . . . only a few lines . . . is double spacing all right?

Definitely. It will give the letter a look of more substance— and should fit better on the page.

INDEX

Abbreviations, names and places, 199

"According to our records," use of "we find" in place of, 79

Action, motivating the reader to, 9, 12, 49, 62, 65–67; in closings, 65–67, 72–76; in collection letters, 95, 99–112; completing letters (WHO–WHAT–WHERE–WHEN–WHY–HOW) to achieve, 48–51, 63; in follow-ups, 134–41; in inquiry letters, 113; making it sound easy to act, 66–67; planning for, 15, 19, 21, 23

Action words, use of, 82. *See also* Active verbs, use of

Active verbs, use of, 13. *See also* Active words, use of

Address (salutation), forms of, 203–5

Adjustment letters, 128–32 (*See also* Complaints); answering, 129–31; examples of, 129–32; guidelines for, 129

Advertising, refusing requests for, 164, 170

"Advise," use of "tell" in place of, 52

"Aggregate," use of "total" or "entire" in place of, 52

"Along the lines of," use of "like" in place of, 53

Anniversaries, congratulatory letters for, 143

Annual Reports, company, answering letters of complaint about duplication of, 127

Apologies (apologetic approach), 17, 19, 37, 42; and admitting mistakes, 37, 42, 61–62, 63, 70–71, 73; in closings, 73–74

Appreciation (appreciative approach), 17, 20, 21, 32 (*See also* Thank-you Notes); expressed in closings, 71

"Are of the opinion," use of "believe" in place of, 53

Arguments, avoiding in replies to customers' complaints, 122, 129

Asking for reader's help and cooperation approach, 22, 23, 36

"As to," use of "about" in place of, 53

"As we previously told you," avoiding use of, 59

"At an early date," avoiding use of (give specific date), 79

"At the present time," use of "now" in place of, 79

Attention-getting (interest-creating) techniques, 23, 25, 49. *See also* Imagination (originality); specific techniques, *e.g.* Curiosity-arousing statements; Humor

Attorneys. *See* Lawsuits

Automobile insurance, answering complaints concerning, 123–24

Awareness of reader's problem, 17, 20, 21, 23, 42. *See also* Sympathetic approach; Understanding approach

Babies, congratulatory letters on birth of, 144–45

Badly written letters, reasons for and how to avoid, 12–13

Banking industry correspondence, 33, 51, 59, 61, 96–97

Beginnings. *See* Openings

"Be in a position to," use of "can" or "able" in place of, 79

Birthday greetings, 146–47

Births, congratulatory letters on, 144–45

"Blahs, The," use of phrase, 81

Blame (blaming the reader) (*See also* Apologies [apologetic approach]; Errors), avoiding, 61, 133–34; in follow-up letters, 133–34

Block paragraph style, 206

Bluntness (curtness), 9 (*See also* Brevity); avoiding in openings, 29; in body of letter, 55; in sentence structure, 55

Body (middle) of letters, 44–63; avoiding technical terms, 45; choice of words in, 45–47; clearness in, 44–45; coherency in, 48; completeness in, 48–52; conciseness in, 52–55; courtesy in, 55–63; grammar in, 47; sentence structure in, 46–47 (*see also* Sentences); use of "you" in, 56–57

Book clubs, making it hard for reader to say "no" to, 67

Brevity (*See also* Bluntness; Conciseness); in collection letters, 96; in follow-ups, 134; in use of words, 46, 52–54, 59–60